P9-CRT-589

SPEND THE DAY IN ANCIENT EGYPT

Projects and Activities
That Bring the Past to Life

Linda Honan

Illustrations by Ellen Kosmer

MEMORIAL
81 CENTRAL AVENUE
HULL, MASSACHUSETTS 02045

John Wiley & Sons, Inc.

New York • Chichester • Weinheim • Brisbane • Singapore • Toronto

This book is printed on acid-free paper. ☉

Copyright © 1999 by Linda Honan. All rights reserved

Illustrations © 1999 by Ellen Kosmer

Published by John Wiley & Sons, Inc.
Published simultaneously in Canada

No part of this publication may be reproduced, stored in a retrieval system, or transmitted in any form or by any means, electronic, mechanical, photocopying, recording, scanning, or otherwise, except as permitted under Section 107 or 108 of the 1976 United States Copyright Act, without either the prior written permission of the Publisher, or authorization through payment of the appropriate per-copy fee to the Copyright Clearance Center, 222 Rosewood Drive, Danvers, MA 01923, (978) 750-8400, fax (978) 750-4744. Requests to the Publisher for permission should be addressed to the Permissions Department, John Wiley & Sons, Inc., 605 Third Avenue, New York, NY 10158-0012, (212) 850-6011, fax (212) 850-6008, e-mail PERMREQ@WILEY.COM.

The publisher and the author have made every reasonable effort to ensure that the experiments and activities in the book are safe when conducted as instructed but assume no responsibility for any damage caused or sustained while performing the experiments or activities in the book. Parents, guardians, and/or teachers should supervise young readers who undertake the experiments and activities in this book.

Library of Congress Cataloging-in-Publication Data

Honan, Linda
    Spend the day in ancient Egypt : projects and activities that bring the past to life / Linda Honan ; illustrated by Ellen Kosmer.
    p.   cm.

    Includes bibliographical references and index.
    Summary: Text, projects, and activities introduce daily life in ancient Egypt from the viewpoint of a fictional family celebrating a festival day in honor of one of their gods.

    ISBN 0-471-29006-8 (paper)

    1. Egypt—Social life and customs—To 332 B.C.—Study and teaching—Activity programs Juvenile literature. [1. Egypt—Social life and customs—To 332B.C.] I. Kosmer, Ellen Virginia, ill. II. Title.

DT61.H67   1999

932—dc21   99-20805

Printed in the United States of America
10 9 8 7 6 5 4

To the Cats in Our Lives:
Seamus, Nevers, Bodley, Crookie, and All

ACKNOWLEDGMENTS

I'd like to thank Professor Leonard Lesko, Brown University, and Henry Robinson, Museum of Science, Boston, for their generous help with some specific questions. To the perspicacious and talented staff at John Wiley & Sons, Inc., especially Kate Bradford and John Simko, my sincere appreciation. And to Kent dur Russel and all the staff, my friends and erstwhile colleagues at Higgins Armory Museum, Worcester, Massachusetts, my unstinting affection and admiration.

—Linda Honan

I very much appreciate the advice and assistance of John Simko, at John Wiley & Sons, Inc. I would also like to acknowledge my feline models and sources of inspiration, Seamus and Nevers, who, at every opportunity involved themselves in helping me with my illustrations.

—Ellen Kosmer

CONTENTS

INTRODUCTION

Welcome to Ancient Egypt!

Wouldn't it be wonderful to wake up in a faraway place where people are working on one of the most exciting projects of all time—the building of a pyramid! In this book you will travel back in time to ancient Egypt, where you will spend a day with a family that might have lived there more than forty-five hundred years ago.

Egypt is a country in North Africa. Its land spreads out on either side of the Nile River, the longest river in the world. Three sources join to form the Nile. The White Nile rises at Lake Victoria in Uganda, the Blue Nile rises in the mountains of Ethiopia, and the Atbara flows into the Nile near Berber. The Nile flows 4,185 miles (6,696 km) north to the Mediterranean Sea. It enters the sea in a marshy region called the Delta, because it is shaped like the Greek letter delta (Δ). The Delta region is called Lower Egypt, while the southern part of the country is called Upper Egypt. Upper Egypt is very hot and dry, while Lower Egypt is warm and has some rain. We will spend the day in the Delta region, at a village on the Giza plateau near modern Cairo. From ancient times, the year in Egypt has been divided into three seasons, based on the annual flood of the Nile River. The flood is caused by heavy summer rains in the mountains of Ethiopia. Each year between June and September the Nile bursts its banks and covers the land on either side. The year begins at this flood season, called *akhet.* Then in October the water level drops and leaves a layer of rich mud in which farmers plant seeds of wheat, barley, and vegetables. This planting season, which lasts from October through February, is called *peret.* From

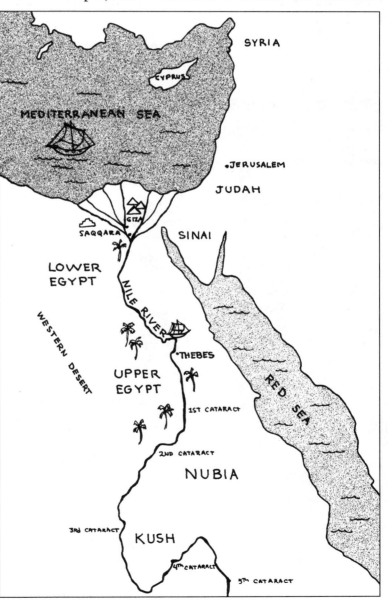

March to May is the season of drought, called *shemu*. This is when the farmers harvest their crops.

We are visiting Egypt at new year or akhet (in our month of July), in the year 2535 B.C. This period in Egyptian history is called the Fourth Dynasty of the Old Kingdom. The kings of Egypt were called **pharaohs,** and they ruled about four million people. At this time the pharaoh was called Cheops (KEE-ops) or Khufu (KOO-foo)—each pharaoh had many names. We are visiting Egypt during the celebration of Cheops's thirtieth jubilee, a special anniversary called the *sed* festival, which was believed to make the pharaoh young again. Cheops is best remembered for having built the largest stone building in the world, the Great Pyramid at Giza, for his tomb. Ancient Egyptians believed that their pharaoh would live forever and protect his people, as long as his body and soul were kept safe in his tomb.

Meet the Family

We are going to spend a day with ten-year-old Meryt and her twelve-year-old brother, Ipy, who live with their mother, Neferure, and their father, Paneb, in Giza. (Egyptians have no family names. Instead, people are identified by their father's or mother's name. So Ipy is known as Ipy-son-of-Paneb or Ipy-son-of-Neferure. Meryt is called Meryt-daughter-of-Paneb or Meryt-daughter-of-Neferure.)

Pashed

Tutu

Ani   Ipy   Paneb   Neferure   Meryt

Paneb is a learned man, a **scribe.** He carries a palm-tree staff called a *bay* to indicate his position. Scribes worked for the state as accountants, administrators, and tax gatherers. Paneb is an important member of the team of architects and builders that is working on Cheops's pyramid.

Ipy has just become Paneb's apprentice and spends most of his time with the pyramid builders. Meryt spends her days at home, helping her mother. Meryt will be married in a couple of years, so she needs to learn all about caring for a family. She also loves music and hopes to become a priestess and spend part of her time singing and playing music in a temple.

Two servants live with the family. Pashed takes care of the family's herd of sheep and cattle, and plants their garden. Tutu helps Neferure in the house, drawing water from the village cistern, doing the laundry, and cooking. They are both paid with goods, since the Egyptians have no money.

Their village is built on land that is raised a few feet above the river valley. This protects it from the annual flood. Their house is built of bricks made from the Nile mud and dried in the sun. It has two floors, a cellar, and a flat roof, where the family spends a lot of time enjoying the breeze from the river. Inside, the house is dark, with one door and small windows. At the back there is a yard with their oven, and a garden with flowers, vegetables, beehives made of papyrus, and trees for shade. Their sheep and cattle live in a pen next to the house. Their cat lives inside with the family.

Egyptians love color and decoration, and their house is painted with bright colors and scenes of daily life. A scene on their living room walls shows the family in a boat on the marsh, hunting water birds with the help of their cat. Another scene shows a party with women dancing and musicians playing.

The Projects and Activities

In this book, you'll follow Ipy and Meryt through their day, and along the way you'll do many of the things that they did. You'll make the kind of clothes and jewelry they wore, write using their hieroglyphs, prepare the kinds of food they ate, and much more. Through these projects and activities, ancient Egypt will come alive. And you'll discover what life was like thousands of years ago for children just like you.

PHARAOH'S TOMB

King Cheops and his priests chose to build his pyramid on the Giza plateau, an area of raised land on the west bank of the Nile near the Delta. The pharaohs built their tombs on the Nile's west bank because the sun sets in the west. The Egyptians believed that each night the sun sails in a boat beneath the earth, traveling from west to east. During the day the sun travels above the earth from east to west across the sky. They believed the dead pharaoh would travel with the sun, so they built his tomb in the west, where the sun began his nightly journey beneath the earth. They called the world underneath the earth the underworld. They believed that dead people lived in the underworld, ruled by the pharaoh. Because the pharaohs' tombs were built on the west bank, the Egyptians called them "houses of the west."

CHAPTER·1

WAKING UP IN GIZA

Dawn comes early on this summer day over the Nile Delta, and Ipy wakes with the sun. His father, Paneb, is shaking his shoulder. Today is a festival day, and the family is looking forward to an evening of celebration and a great feast in honor of the pharaoh at the temple of the goddess Bastet. But before they can enjoy the holiday, they have a busy day ahead of them.

Egyptian children spend their first years playing, so that they will grow up to be healthy and strong. As soon as they are able, they begin to help with their parents' work. Now that she is ten, Meryt helps her mother at home. Ipy has just turned twelve and has been accepted at the school for scribes, where he will learn his father's trade. Scribes are highly trained officials who work for the pharaoh (the king) or for other important people. Today, Paneb and Ipy must go to the pyramid site to check on a boatload of stone that is being delivered. Meryt must get ready to play the harp at the festival in the temple of Bastet. Neferure and Tutu must make the house clean and neat for the celebration. Later the whole family will enjoy going fishing in the Delta to catch the food for their feast. Until recently, Ipy didn't need to wear any clothes. None of the children at his school wore any! But now that he is an apprentice scribe he wants to look professional, so he wears a neat skirt. Ipy pulls on his kilt and slips his feet into sandals made of papyrus reed. Like all the boys he knows, Ipy has had most of his hair shaved off, leaving just one long braid hanging over his right ear. He smooths his hair and hangs his lucky scarab *amulet* (charm) around his neck. Hearing Paneb calling him, he runs down to the kitchen for a piece of barley bread and a drink of water. Then he follows Paneb out of the house for the walk to the pyramid site.

ACTIVITY
BOY'S KILT

In this activity you'll make the kind of kilt that Egyptian boys and men wore. Try to find cloth that is a creamy-white color, like the undyed linen the Egyptians used.

MATERIALS

scissors
white sheet, tablecloth, or fabric remnant 3 feet by 18 inches
  (1 m by 45 cm)
yardstick (meterstick)
2 diaper pins or large safety pins
iron (optional)
adult helper (if using iron)

1. Cut a 6-by-18-inch (15-by-45-cm) strip from the cloth, as shown. This will make the apron.

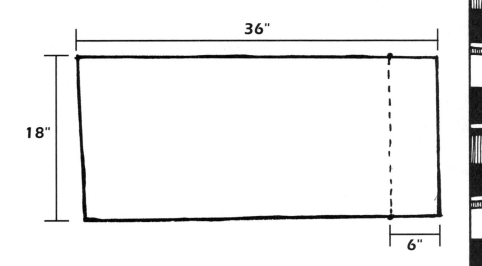

2. Starting at your left hip, wrap the remaining cloth around your waist. Overlap the front so that the kilt ends at your right hip. If there is too much cloth, cut off the excess and discard it.

THE PYRAMID VILLAGE

Architects and engineers, stonecutters and sculptors, carpenters and painters, all worked and lived together in Ipy's village. They came here to build the pyramid and its temples, a huge project that would take them twenty years to finish. Along with the pyramid-builders lived all the people who kept the village going, including farmers and gardeners, cooks and laundry workers, and doctors and teachers. After the pyramid was completed, the village remained so that priests, scribes, and other workers could live there and tend the pyramid and the dead pharaoh.

3. Lay the larger piece of cloth out flat. Use the pins to mark a point 6 inches (15 cm) in from each end along the lower edge.

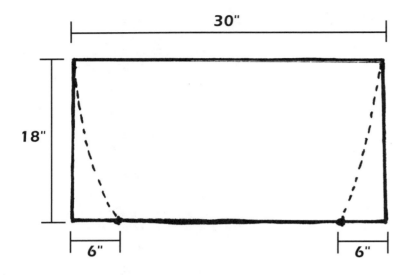

4. Cut a curving line from each pin to the upper corner. Remove the pins.

5. (Optional) Fold your kilt in half, and in half again, four times. Have your adult helper iron the folded kilt to make pleats. Fold and iron the apron in the same way.

6. Put on the kilt. Use the pins to fasten the apron to both thicknesses of cloth.

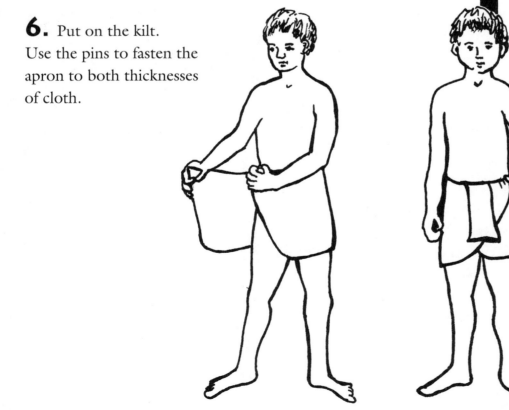

Ankh Amulet

The **ankh** is the Egyptian symbol for life. In Egyptian art, pharaohs are shown carrying an ankh. Ordinary Egyptians wore an ankh amulet to protect them from harm. It was believed to be a powerful magic force. The Egyptians often made the ankh amulet from real gold. Make your own ankh in this activity, then wear it around your neck.

MATERIALS

several sheets of newspaper
½ pound (200 gm) of self-hardening clay (about the size of an orange)
craft stick or modeling tool
pencil
water jar
18-inch (45-cm) piece of string or cord
paintbrush (optional)
blue or gold poster paint (optional)

1. Spread the newspaper over your work area.

2. Work the clay in your hands until it is soft and warm. Pull off a small piece of clay about the size of a plum. Set the small piece aside.

3. Roll the remaining clay on the newspaper into a round shape like a big marble. Flatten the clay into a rectangle 3 inches (7.5 cm) tall by 2 inches (5 cm) wide by ¼ inch (0.6 cm) thick (about as thick as the pencil). Use the craft stick to cut away some clay to make a cross shape as shown on page 10. Use the pencil to make a hole in the top of the cross shape.

EGYPTIAN CLOTHES

Because of the hot climate, people in Egypt did not wear heavy clothes. Younger children wore nothing at all, while older children and adults wore simple clothing made from linen (cloth made from the flax plant). Men wore a loincloth or kilt, and women wore a long, narrow gown. Royal ladies wore gowns made from linen that was so fine it was almost transparent, while workmen wore simple skirts made from coarse linen. Royal and noble people wore linen that was finely pleated. They made the pleats by pressing the wet cloth onto a grooved board and letting it dry. The cloth was left its natural color, a creamy white. In cooler weather or for formal events, men and women wore a linen or woolen shawl that was often fringed.

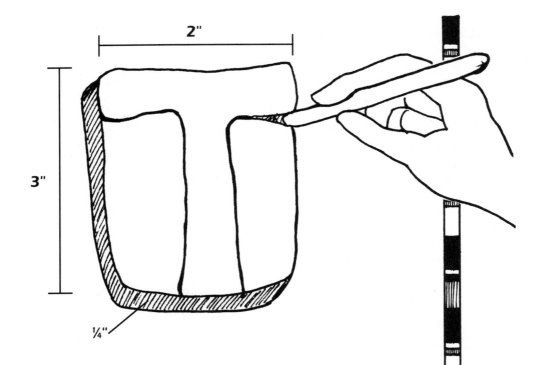

2"

3"

¼"

4. Take the small piece of clay you set aside in step 2. Roll it into a snake shape.

5. Dip your finger in the water jar and wet the ends of the snake. Shape the piece into an oval as shown, and press it gently to the crosspieces of the ankh so it sticks.

6. Smooth the surface of the clay with the craft stick or your fingers to remove any holes or lines as shown. Use the pencil to lightly press in lines.

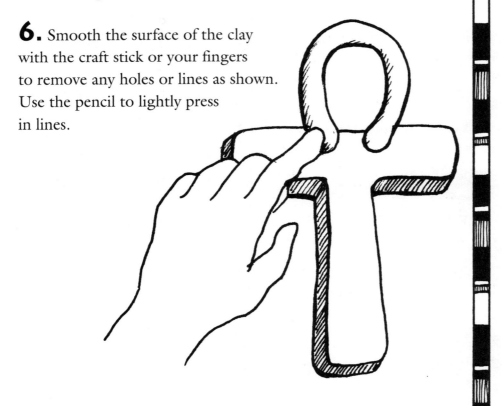

7. Leave the ankh on a piece of clean newspaper while it is drying, as it will leave a stain while wet. Let it dry for two days indoors, away from radiators, sunny windows, or other sources of heat.

8. (Optional) When the ankh is dry, you can paint it gold or blue.

9. Run the cord through the hole in the ankh, and tie the ends in a knot. Now wear your ankh around your neck!

Meryt wakes up almost as early as Ipy. Her bed has a wooden frame with beautiful carved legs shaped like those of an ox. A rush mat supports the mattress, which is a linen cushion. Meryt straightens the linen blanket and pulls on a gown and her papyrus sandals. She combs her hair, then goes to the kitchen to get some breakfast. Nibbling on a piece of barley bread and honey, Meryt goes out to the yard, where Neferure and Tutu are pleating the gowns they will all wear at the festival. Their new cat, Ani, comes over purring, and rubs against Meryt's legs, and Meryt pats his head. In honor of the festival, Ani is wearing gold earrings. Meryt says a morning prayer to their statue of Bes, the dwarf god who is honored in every home. Then she starts to help her mother.

BES

The god Bes was a favorite with all Egyptians even though he had no temple of his own. Instead, many people had statues of him in their homes. Bes was part dwarf and part lion, and is often shown wearing a lion skin around his neck. He looked after babies and brought joy to all the family.

ACTIVITY

PLEATED GOWN

The usual dress of older girls and women in Egypt was an ankle-length white linen gown. The gown was sleeveless. It sometimes had square shoulder straps. The gown was usually pleated. Egyptians wore a shawl over the gown in cooler weather. Make your own pleated gown in this activity.

MATERIALS

3-yard-by-36-inch (270-by-90-cm) white sheet, tablecloth, or
   length of cloth
yardstick (meterstick)
scissors
iron
adult helper

1. Cut a strip 2 by 36 inches (5 by 90 cm) from the cloth. This will be a belt.

2. Fold the cloth in half so it is about 1½ yards (135 cm) long.

3. Cut an 8-by-6-inch (20-by-15-cm) opening for your head at the fold as shown.

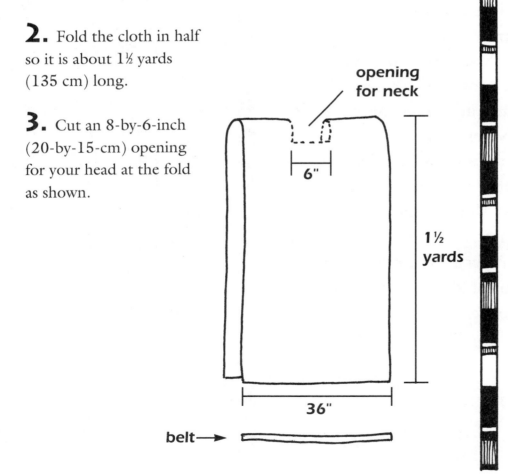

opening for neck

6"

1½ yards

36"

belt →

4. Fold the gown in half the long way, and then in half again. Repeat twice.

5. Ask your adult helper to iron the gown to make the pleats.

6. Put the gown on, and tie the belt under your arms.

ACTIVITY

SCARAB

A scarab is a kind of beetle called a "dung beetle." The Egyptians believed the scarab beetle was sacred to Re and made many beautiful images of the scarab from precious stones. Blue and green were two of the Egyptians' favorite colors for jewelry. Much of their jewelry was made from the blue stone called "lapis lazuli," and from turquoise, which is a blue-green stone. In this activity you can make a handsome scarab from clay.

THE GODS OF EGYPT

The Egyptians worshiped hundreds of different gods. The sun god Re was the most powerful, and he took many different forms. At dawn he was Khepri, a scarab beetle rolling the sun's disk over the edge of the horizon; at noon he was Horus, a hawk; and at sunset he was Atum, a ram-headed man.

Egyptian gods often took the form of animals, or of men or women with animal heads. Sobek was a crocodile god, Bastet a cat, Hathor a cow or cow-headed woman, Thoth an ibis, Khnum a ram, Wadjyt a cobra goddess, Nekhbet a vulture goddess, and Anubis a jackal. Many animals were considered sacred because of their association with a god.

MATERIALS

several sheets of newspaper
¼ pound (100 gm) of self-hardening clay (about the size of a plum)
craft stick or modeling tool
pencil
water jar
18-inch (45-cm) piece of string or cord
paintbrush (optional)
green or blue poster paint (optional)

1. Spread the newspaper over your work area.

2. Squeeze the clay in your hands until it is soft and warm.

3. Roll the clay on the newspaper into a round shape like a marble. Flatten it into an oval 1 ¼ inches (3 cm) tall by ½ inch (1.25 cm) wide by ¼ inch (0.6 cm) thick—about as thick as the pencil.

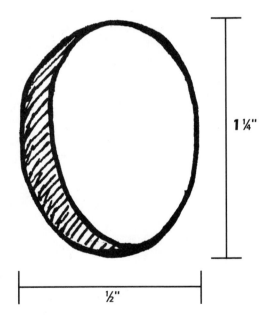

1 ¼"

½"

4. Smooth the surface of the clay with the craft stick or your fingers to remove any holes or lines. Use the pencil to lightly press in lines for the beetle's head and body as shown on page 15.

5. Press the pencil through one end of the scarab to make a hole.

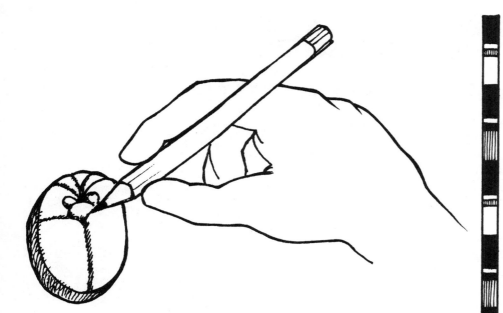

6. Leave the scarab on a piece of clean newspaper while it is drying, as it will leave a stain while wet. Let it dry for two days indoors, away from radiators, sunny windows, or other sources of heat.

7. (Optional) When the scarab is dry, you can paint it blue or green.

8. Run the cord through the hole in the scarab, and tie the ends in a knot. Now wear your scarab around your neck!

CHAPTER 2

IPY MEETS THE PYRAMID BUILDERS

Ipy has just turned twelve, and today is his first day of work as an apprentice scribe. He will spend the next four or five years as an apprentice and then will become a scribe himself. On this festival morning, many people have a holiday and are staying at home, but Paneb and Ipy must go to work for a few hours. The masons are bringing a barge full of stone to the pyramid site, and Paneb and Ipy must be there to check that the correct amount is delivered.

Paneb and Ipy greet their neighbors as they hurry down the raised path that leads to the Nile. The river valley that the Nile floods varies in width from about 1 mile (1.6 km) to 12 miles (19 km). In the Delta, the Nile divides into five major streams, and the fertile area stretches more than 100 miles (160 km) across. The ancient Egyptians called this fertile valley the *Kemet* or Black Land. They called the dry desert on either side of the Kemet the *Deshret* or Red Land. Because of the color of these lands, the Egyptians regarded black as a lucky color and red as an unlucky color. The fertile Black Land near the river is divided into many small fields by ditches. The fields and ditches fill with water during the flood season. After the flood, the water drains away from the fields but stays in the ditches. Farmers take water from the ditches to grow their crops. On this day in mid-July, the floodwaters have already covered the fields that are closest to the river.

A dock has been built near the pyramid. When Paneb and Ipy arrive, the barge full of granite is being towed into place at the dock, after its 500-mile (800-km) journey from Aswan. The foreman of the barge crew greets Paneb, who introduces Ipy as a new apprentice. Ipy feels very important! The dock is filled with busy people. Hundreds of workmen are bringing up big wooden logs on which they will move the huge stones.

PYRAMID STYLE

The tombs of the early pharaohs were made from mud bricks and shaped like big benches. This kind of tomb is called a **mastaba**, which means "bench" in Arabic. Later the Egyptians piled smaller stone mastabas on top of larger ones, to make a rough pyramid shape, with big steps up to the top. This is called a **step pyramid**. Finally, they filled in the steps with an outer cover of stone, making a smooth-sided pyramid like Cheops's. More than thirty pyramids still stand in Egypt. The Great Pyramid at Giza is 481 feet (146 m) high, and each side measures 800 feet (230 m) long.

Paneb tells Ipy to count the blocks as they are brought off the barge. Ipy checks them off on a piece of clay called an ostrakon. Then Paneb asks Ipy to help him measure each block with a cubit stick, to make sure that they are the right size.

ACTIVITY

EGYPTIAN NUMBERS

Egyptian numbers were based on units of 10. There was no 0. The Egyptians used addition and subtraction to solve all their math problems; they did not use multiplication or division. Try your hand at writing Egyptian numbers, then figure out what numbers Ipy must write down. Write the answers in Egyptian notation, then check them against the answers printed at the bottom of page 19.

NUMBERS	HIEROGLYPH
1	
10	
100	
1,000	
10,000	
100,000	
1,000,000	

Paneb tells Ipy that 2,300,000 blocks of stone will be needed to build the pyramid. Each boat brings 100 blocks of stone and travels 1,000 miles (1,600 km) from Aswan to Giza and back.

1. **(a)** Ipy is 12, **(b)** Meryt is 10, and **(c)** their new cat, Ani, is 2. Write down their ages in Egyptian numbers.

2. Write out 2,300,000 as Ipy would.

3. How many trips will the boats have to make from Aswan to Giza?

4. How many miles/kilometers will the boats cover on all these trips?

Answers

1a.  1b. 1c.

2.

3.

4.

miles

or

km.

IMHOTEP

Imhotep was an important official called a **vizier.** The vizier was the highest official in Egypt under the pharaoh. Imhotep worked for King Djoser (2630–2611 B.C.). Imhotep is remembered as the patron of architects and as a great healer. He built the first stone pyramid, a step pyramid at Saqqara. He was such a skilled craftsman that he was said to be the son of Ptah, the god of craftsmen.

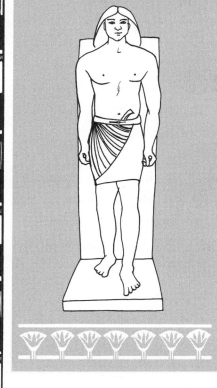

ACTIVITY
CUBIT STICK

A cubit stick is an ancient measuring stick that is based on the unit called a **cubit**, which was the distance from the tip of your middle finger to your elbow. The **hieroglyph** (Egyptian picture-writing sign) for a cubit is a forearm. The standard Egyptian measuring stick was called the **royal cubit**. It is 20⅝ inches (52.4 cm) long. The cubit was divided into seven **palms** (the width of a hand), and each palm was divided into four **thumbs.** So the cubit was divided into twenty-eight thumbs, each about ¾ inch (2 cm) long. Make your own cubit stick in this activity, and use it to measure the pyramid you will build!

MATERIALS
paper grocery bag or a 17-by-12-inch (43-by-30-cm) piece of
  brown paper
scissors
stapler
pencil
ruler

1. Cut down the sides of the paper bag and across the bottom to make a 17-by-12-inch (43-by-30-cm) rectangle. Discard the rest of the bag.

2. Fold the paper in half the long way. Repeat twice, to make a strip that is 17 by 1½ inches (43 by 3.75 cm). Staple along the fold.

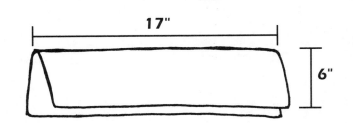

3. Lay your forearm on top of the paper, with your elbow at one end. Stretch out your fingers, and use the pencil to mark where your middle fingertip ends. This is your cubit length.

4. Measure your cubit with the ruler. Divide your cubit length by 7, and mark off the seven palms.

5. Now divide each palm by 4, and mark off each thumb. Now you have your own cubit stick to measure with!

Standing on the dock under the hot sun, Ipy watches the workmen unload the huge stone blocks. It is really hard work, but the workmen are cheerful. They work in teams and compete to see which team is fastest. Sometimes they ask a scribe to write the team's name on the bottom of a block they have moved.

After Ipy has counted and measured all the blocks, Paneb lets him go to where a priest and his assistant are measuring the depth of the Nile with a nilometer. A nilometer is a gauge carved on stone

HOW THEY BUILT THE PYRAMIDS

The workers had no cranes or pulleys to help move the stone blocks, each of which weighed more than 2 tons (2,000 kg). Instead, they built a mud ramp all around the sides of the pyramid. Teams of men pushed each block onto a wooden sled that moved up the ramp on rollers. As the pyramid grew higher, the men built the ramp around it higher, too, so they could keep adding more stone blocks to the walls. When the pyramid's four walls had reached up to meet at a point, the builders put on the capstone. This was a stone shaped like a pyramid and covered in gold. Then the builders covered all the walls of the pyramid with a thin layer of especially beautiful stone. They built this outer layer from the top down. As they worked, they pulled down the mud ramp that surrounded the pyramid.

steps set in the banks of the Nile. By noting how high the water is each month, the priests can foretell how high the floodwaters will rise each year. This information is very important to all Egyptians. If the water is too low, not enough land will be flooded for the planting season, and people will go hungry. But if the flood is too high, their houses will be washed away. By keeping careful track of the height of the Nile, the people can try to plan ahead for the next flood season.

ACTIVITY

PYRAMID

A pyramid is a four-sided, three-dimensional structure with the sides meeting in a point. The base of the pyramid is square. Make your own pyramid, and use your cubit stick to measure it.

MATERIALS

pencil
ruler
18-by-24-inch (45-by-60-cm) piece of construction paper
protractor
scissors
white glue
cubit stick

1. Use the pencil and ruler to draw a line from each corner of your paper through the center to the opposite corner. Where the two lines cross is the center point. Mark it X.

2. Measure a point 3 inches (7.5 cm) out from the X on each of the four lines. Draw a square connecting these points.

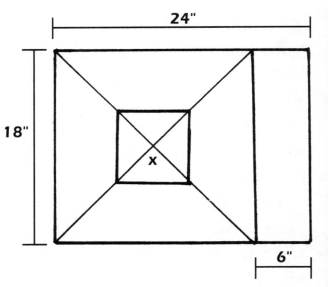

3. Use the protractor and ruler to measure a 60-degree angle on the outer side of each point of your square. Extend the line along the angle to form a triangle.

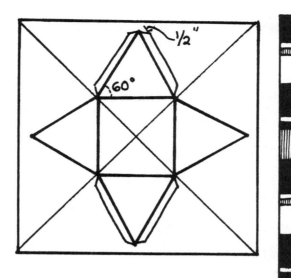

4. On two facing triangles, rule a line ½ inch (1.25 cm) out from the lines to make a flap. Cut out your pyramid.

5. Fold the four base lines up. Crease the flaps upward, and fold the pyramid. Glue the flaps to the sides.

6. Use your cubit stick to measure the height of each side of your pyramid.

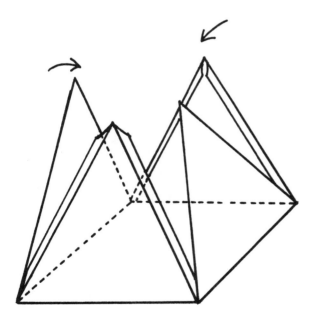

INSIDE A PYRAMID

The inside of Cheops's pyramid is made of solid stone. A couple of secret passages lead to some small rooms where the pharaoh is buried and where priests will come to make offerings. The pyramid must have everything the pharaoh will need for a happy afterlife—priests, servants, animals, food, incense, and music. Since live servants and real food could not last forever, the Egyptians made models of people (called **shabti** or **ushabti** figures) and of food and animals to stay in the pyramid. They painted the walls with scenes the pharaoh enjoyed—his family listening to music, feasting in a garden, or hunting in the Delta. Real furniture, jewelry, and musical instruments were put in the pyramid for the pharaoh to use.

CHAPTER 3

MERYT'S MUSIC LESSON

Like many Egyptian women, Neferure worked as a priestess for a year before she was married. She was a musician in the temple of Bastet, the cat goddess. Ten-year-old Meryt studies music because she hopes to become a priestess, too. Meryt is excited because she has been chosen to sing and play the harp in the temple during the festival of Bastet today. After breakfast, Meryt has a music lesson with her mother, practicing the pieces she will play this afternoon.

The harp is in their living room, the biggest room in the house. It is cool, with thick walls and a high ceiling held up by pillars called columns. Lotus flowers are carved around the tops of the columns, which are called capitals. The chairs and tables in the room are decorated with thin layers of gold and colored with stones and paint. Besides the harp, they have other musical instruments. Ipy plays a double flute, and Meryt plays a rattle called a *sistrum*

and another instrument called a *menat*, which is a string of beads shaken to sound a beat. When they are not playing instruments, the family sometimes relaxes by playing a board game called *senet*.

ACTIVITY

SENET

Senet, or Passing, is one of the oldest board games in the world. Two sets made of ebony wood and ivory were buried with the pharaoh Tutankhamun. The board on which senet was played was also the box that held the pieces. Use your senet box to hold other small toys if you like.

MATERIALS

several sheets of newspaper
shoe box
five 9-by-12-inch (23-by-30-cm) sheets of white or tan
  construction paper
pencil
ruler
scissors

white glue

two 9-by-12-inch (23-by-30-cm) sheets of black or brown
*   construction paper*

4 craft sticks

½ pound (200 gm) of self-hardening clay (about the size of an
*   orange)*

black marker

red marker

blue and red paint

paintbrush

water jar

TO MAKE THE GAME BOARD

1. Cover your work space with the newspaper.

2. Take the shoe box. Trace each surface of the box on the white paper. Cut out the pieces, and glue them to the box.

3. Stand the lid along the edge of the sheet of black paper. Mark the length of the lid. Measure a strip 2 inches (5 cm) wide by the length of the lid. Cut it out.

4. Fold the strip you just cut in half the long way, and cut it along the fold. Fold the two strips in half again the long way, and cut along the folds to get four thin strips.

5. Stand the lid along the edge of the sheet of black paper. Mark the width of the lid. Use the ruler and pencil to measure eleven strips ½ inch (1.25 cm) wide by the width of the lid. Cut them out.

6. Find the center point along the long side of the lid. Mark it with the pencil. Squeeze a thin line of glue on one of the eleven strips of black paper, and press it across the lid along this center line. Repeat with two more strips at each narrow end.

7. Measure the space between the center strip and one of the end strips. Divide this amount into five sections, and glue a black paper strip to mark five equal spaces. Repeat at the other end of the lid.

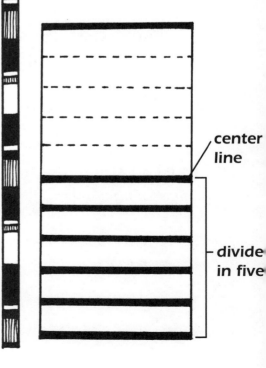

center
line

divide
in five

8. Take two of the long strips of black paper you made in steps 3 and 4, and glue them along the long sides of the lid. Measure the width of the lid, and divide it into three sections. Glue the other two long strips of black paper to mark three equal spaces.

9. Mark the lucky and unlucky squares on the board. Remember, to the Egyptians, black is a lucky color and red is unlucky! Mark the squares shown in the illustration. Use the black marker to write the Egyptian numerals two and three; when someone lands on these, they must throw a 2 or 3 to reach the last square. Use the red marker to mark the wavy line that means "water," and the cross that means "crossing" or "damage." Whoever lands on the water is said to have drowned, and that piece is taken off the board and must begin again at the start. A piece that lands on the X must move backward the same number that the player last threw.

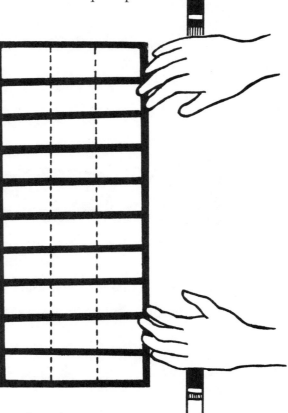

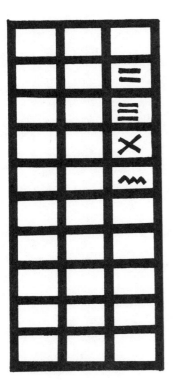

TO MAKE THE GAME PIECES

1. Work the clay in your hands until it is soft and warm. Divide the clay in half. Set half of it aside.

2. Divide the other half of the clay into four equal pieces, each about the size of a strawberry. Shape each piece into a cone. Make sure the bottoms are flat so they can stand.

3. Take the other half of the clay, and divide it into four equal pieces. Roll each piece into a ball, then flatten the balls into a disk shape.

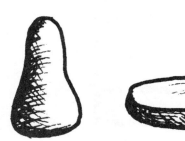

4. Leave the game pieces on a piece of clean newspaper while they are drying, as they will leave a stain while wet. Let them dry for two days indoors, away from radiators, sunny windows, or other sources of heat.

5. When they are dry, paint the cones red and the disks blue.

TO MAKE THE THROW STICKS

1. Take the craft sticks, and paint one of the hieroglyphs shown here (or another hieroglyph) on one side of each craft stick.

HOW TO PLAY SENET

Two players sit facing each other at each long end of the board. The object is to be the first player to move all your men around the board. The squares on the board with a black number are lucky, and if you land on them, you move forward as many squares as the number. The squares with a red number are unlucky, and if you land on them, you must fall back as many squares as the number. One player has the cone playing pieces, and the other has the disks.

Each player throws all four throwing sticks up in the air. When they land, count how many of the hieroglyphs you can see. If you can see one, then the player's score is 1. If you can see four, then the player's score is 4, and so on.

Whoever gets the higher score at the first throw starts the game by putting his first man on the lucky corner square. The players throw the sticks in turn and move the amount they score. If they land on a black hieroglyphic square, they add the score indicated. If they land on a red hieroglyphic square, they subtract the score indicated. Each time a player scores 4, he may put another man on the board. The men are moved all around the outer edge of the board and then up the center to end at the hieroglyphic square. You must throw the right number to land on this lucky square.

Neferure kneels to play the harp, which is nearly four feet high. Meryt sings the songs she is learning. Some of them are religious, and some are cheerful, popular songs. When she has gone over her songs, Meryt plays the harp pieces she will perform this afternoon. She is still learning, and it does not sound as sweet as when her mother plays. Neferure tells her she is getting better all the time and encourages her to keep practicing.

They finish up with Meryt playing the sistrum, a kind of rattle, while her mother plays the harp.

OSIRIS AND ISIS

Osiris and Isis were important gods of the underworld, where dead souls lived. Osiris was a king of Egypt who was murdered by his brother Seth. Their sister Isis, who was also Osiris's wife, rescued his body and brought him back to life. Osiris and Isis are usually shown in human form, but Isis is also shown as a bird called a kite.

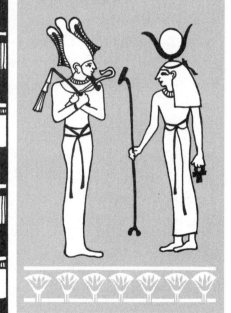

Tutu comes in from the yard and claps her hands and sways to the music. Soon Meryt joins her, and they dance all around the room, singing a song of praise to Hathor, the goddess of music!

ACTIVITY

SISTRUM

The sistrum (plural, *sistra*) is a musical instrument like a rattle. Priestesses played it in the temples of ancient Egypt, and it is still used today during services in the Coptic Christian church of Egypt. Sistra were often decorated with images of the goddess Hathor.

MATERIALS

wire clothes hanger
2 feet (60 cm) of florist's wire
24 tabs from pop-top cans, or brass paper fasteners
6-by-4-inch (15-by-10-cm) piece of cardboard
pencil
colored markers
duct tape

1. Take a wire clothes hanger, and pull down on the center hanging bar until it is bent into a U shape.

2. Squeeze the hook of the hanger closed to make a handle as shown on page 31.

3. Cut the florist's wire into three equal parts. Take one piece of the wire and tie one end to the hanger, halfway up the loop. Wrap the wire around the hanger several times. Thread eight tabs or fasteners on this wire. (If you use fasteners, bend their ends around the wire.) Tie the other end of the wire to the hanger.

4. Take the second piece of wire and tie one end to the hanger, 1 inch (2.5 cm) above the first wire. Thread eight tabs or fasteners on this wire. (If you use fasteners, bend their ends around the wire.) Tie the other end of the wire to the hanger.

5. Take the third piece of wire and tie one end to the hanger, 1 inch (2.5 cm) above the second wire. Thread eight tabs or fasteners on this wire. Tie the other end of the wire to the hanger.

6. On the cardboard, draw a 2½-inch (6.25-cm) sun disk with the horns of the goddess Hathor. Below the disk, draw a handle 1 inch (2.5 cm) wide by 3 inches (7.5 cm) long. Color the disk and horns with the markers. Cut out the disk, horns, and handle.

7. Place the Hathor badge on top of the handle of the sistrum. Wrap the badge and handle in the duct tape.

8. Now play your sistrum in time to a song you can sing!

ACTIVITY

MENAT RHYTHM BEADS

Another way that Egyptians kept time to their music was by shaking a string of beads called a *menat*. Make your own menat with colorful beads.

MATERIALS

20 round beads in various colors
2-foot (60-cm) piece of string

1. Arrange your beads in a colorful pattern.

2. Tie a triple knot 3 inches (7.5 cm) from one end of the string.

3. Thread the beads on the string.

4. Tie the ends of the string together.

5. Now use your menat to beat a rhythm!

ACTIVITY
TOY LION

Egyptian children played with many kinds of toys. They had dolls made of wood or papyrus with hair made of balls of mud. They also had toy animals such as lions and hippopotamuses. Some of these toys had parts that moved, like the lion you can make in this activity.

MATERIALS

2 pieces of heavy paper or thin cardboard, one about 8 by 8 inches
(20 by 20 cm) and one 4 by 8 inches (10 by 20 cm)
pencil
scissors
3 brass paper fasteners
colored pencils or markers
paper punch

1. On the larger piece of paper or cardboard, draw a lion walking, seen from the side. Show only the near legs of the lion, one front leg and one back leg, as shown in the drawing.

2. Cut out your lion.

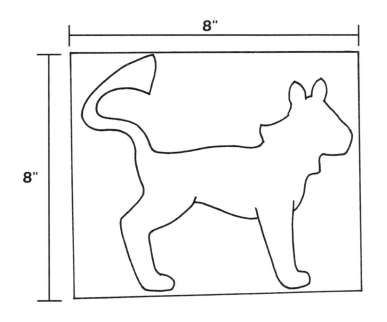

8"

8"

MA'AT

The quality that ancient Egyptians valued most is called **ma'at**. This means good behavior, honesty, and justice. Ma'at is also the name of the goddess of truth, who is shown as a woman with a feather or wings like an angel. After death, Ma'at weighed every Egyptian's heart against her feather. If someone had been wicked, his heart was heavier than her feather, and he was taken away by demons. But if he had been good, his heart was light and he would live forever in a happy afterlife.

3. Trace around the legs of the lion on the smaller piece of paper or cardboard. Cut out these legs.

4. Trace around the lower jaw of the lion on the smaller piece of paper or cardboard. Cut out this jaw.

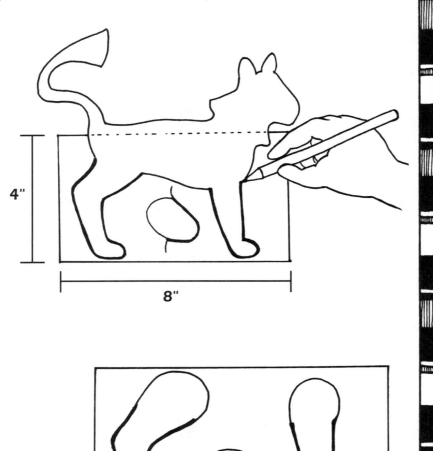

5. Place the new front leg right on top of the old front leg. Use the paper punch to make a hole ½ inch (1.25 cm) down from the top of the legs. Fasten the legs together with the paper fastener.

6. Follow the same procedure to fasten the new back leg over the old back leg and the new jaw over the old jaw.

7. Color the lion, and draw the lion's mane, eyes, and whiskers with the pencils or markers.

8. Move the lion's legs and jaw to make him seem to walk and roar.

CHAPTER·4

IPY VISITS
THE HOUSE OF LIFE

Paneb finds Ipy, and they walk together up the raised path to the pyramid site. A stone wall all around keeps out animals and people who don't belong there. Inside the wall there are several big buildings. Everything connected with the pharaoh's pyramid is huge!

Three smaller pyramids are being built for the queen and the princes and princesses. The vizier, scribes, and other important people who work for the pharaoh will be buried here, too. There are also three temples, offices, workshops, and the school for scribes, which is called the House of Life.

The entrance gate is in the east wall. The first build- ing inside the gate is the mortuary temple. This is where priests will *embalm* (pre- serve with chem- icals) the pharaoh's body and *mummify* it (dry it out with salt) for its eternal life in the pyra- mid. The priests who designed the pyramid placed it so that two of its sides face exactly east to west and the other two face north to south. At the gate to the mortuary temple there are tall, slanting pil- lars called *pylons*. Ipy has never been inside the gate before. He looks up at the pylons and is amazed. He can hardly believe that from tomorrow, he will be coming here every day.

The House of Life, the school where the student scribes spend most of their time, is near the mortu- ary temple. Paneb unlocks the door and shows Ipy the classroom. Ipy sees where he will sit on the floor to study, and where the boards and brushes and ink that he will be using are kept. The master sits on a beautiful carved and painted stool. Ipy knows he is lucky to be an apprentice scribe. Many boys would like to attend the House of Life, but only the sons of scribes may become students here.

When he starts school tomorrow, Ipy will spend his days practicing writing on wooden boards coat- ed with plaster, using a brush made from reeds and

THOTH

Thoth was the messenger of the gods, and the **patron** (protector) of scribes and of learning. He was shown as a man with the head of an ibis (a bird with a long, thin beak), holding a scribe's brush and **palette**, the tray on which he mixed ink with water. Before an Egyptian scribe wrote anything, he always poured out some of this water as an offering to Thoth. Thoth was some- times shown as a baboon, and both the ibis and the baboon were sacred to him. Thousands of ibis and baboons were mummified and buried near Thoth's temple at Khemenu (also called Hermopolis) in Upper Egypt.

ink made from soot. When he wants to write something important that is meant to last, he will write on papyrus, a kind of paper made from a reed that grows in the Delta.

Egyptian writing in Ipy's day is made up of hieroglyphs instead of letters. Hieroglyphs are simplified pictures that stand for a word or a sound. Ipy has to learn more than seven hundred of them! This is why it takes so long to become a scribe, and why Ipy has to work so hard—but also why he will be given so much respect when he succeeds.

ACTIVITY

HIEROGLYPHS

Hieroglyphs can be written vertically, one underneath the other, and are always read from the top down. They can also be written horizontally and may be read either from left to right or from right to left. You can tell which way to read a horizontal line of hieroglyphs by the way in which the faces in the hieroglyphic pictures are facing. You always read from the face to the back of the head!

There are no spaces between the words in hieroglyphic writing, so it is hard to tell where one word ends and the next begins. However, names of gods and pharaohs and queens and important people are written inside an oval line called a *cartouche*. For beginning readers, these names are the easiest Egyptian words to read! This example shows the name of Cleopatra:

As you can see from the animals' faces, you read this name from left to right.

Here are two other examples of Egyptian names:

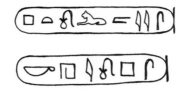

Here are some useful hieroglyphs that can be used for English letters.

a		j		s	
b		k		t	
c		l		u	
d		m		v	
e		n		w	
f		o		x	
g		p		y	
h		q		z	
i		r			

Using these hieroglyphs, try your hand at writing these English names.

Mary

John

Now try writing your own name! Don't forget to enclose your name in a cartouche, since you are certainly an important person!

ACTIVITY

PAPYRUS SCROLL

The Egyptians had no books like ours. When they wanted to write a long text, they wrote it on a papyrus scroll. Make your own scroll and write a message on it in hieroglyphics!

MATERIALS
several sheets of newspaper
plastic bowl
1 cup (0.25 l) of water

HIEROGLYPHS

The ancient Egyptian system of writing is called hieroglyphics, and each sign is called a hieroglyph. Hieroglyphs developed about 3,000 B.C. and may have started as early wall paintings. They are made up of simple drawings that stand for things and also for the sounds of words. Only the consonants are shown (b, c, d, f, g, and so on), not the vowels (a, e, i, o, u). Because of this, they are hard to read. Unlike our alphabet of twenty-six letters, there are more than seven hundred different hieroglyphs!

1 tablespoon (15 ml) of white glue
plastic spoon
2 thick paper towels, in plain white
scissors
6 to 10 grasses, either lawn grass or wild grass
plastic wrap, about 14 by 11 inches (35 by 27.5 cm)
paints and brush
12-inch (30-cm) piece of string

1. Spread the newspaper over your work area.

2. Pour the glue and water into the bowl. Mix them with the spoon.

3. Cut the paper towels into strips ½ inch (1.25 cm) wide.

4. Put the paper strips into the water and glue. Add the grasses.

5. Spread the plastic wrap out on the newspaper. Carefully take one paper strip from the glue mixture. Spread it out from side to side on the plastic.

6. Take another strip of paper from the bowl. Spread it out on the plastic from front to back so that the end covers one end of the first strip.

7. Continue to overlap the strips like this until you have used them all. The numbers in the illustration below show in what order to place the strips.

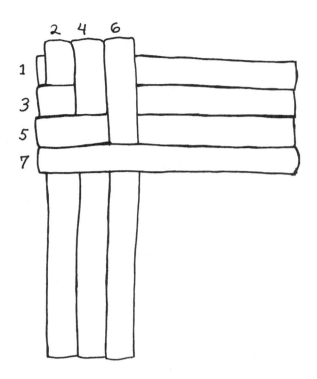

8. Take the grasses and scatter them over the paper.

9. Press down the strips with your finger to make them flat. Let your papyrus dry overnight.

10. Peel off the plastic. Now paint a hieroglyph or Egyptian design on your papyrus! When it is dry, roll up your scroll and tie the string around it.

ROSETTA STONE

For nearly two thousand years after the Egyptian Empire ended, people forgot how to read hieroglyphics. Then in 1822, French scholar Jean-François Champollion studied a stone found at Rosetta, a town in the Delta. There were three kinds of ancient writing on the stone: Greek, hieroglyphics, and demotic (a simplified Egyptian alphabet).

Champollion guessed that the same message was written in all three scripts. He knew how to read Greek and compared that text to the other two in order to understand them. Once he realized that any word within a cartouche was a name, he was able to figure out the hieroglyphs spelling Ptolemy and Cleopatra. This led him to solve the meaning of the other hieroglyphs.

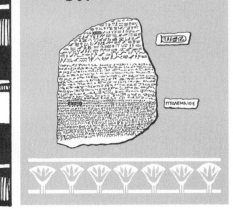

ACTIVITY

OBELISK

Egyptian obelisks were colossal pillars raised outside temples. Today many people like to have a small obelisk on a desk or table. Make an obelisk as a gift, and write the owner's name in a cartouche running down the side!

MATERIALS

white poster board 28 by 18 inches (70 by 45 cm)
pencil
ruler
drawing compass
scissors
protractor
glue
colored markers

1. Turn the poster board over, and work on the back of the board. Use the pencil and ruler to find the middle point of each of the short sides. Draw a line to connect these points, A-B.

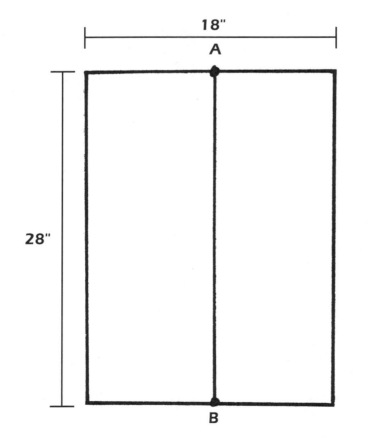

2. Measure 1¾ inches (4.5 cm) back from A along your line A-B. Mark this point X. Draw a 1¾-inch (4.5-cm) line at a right angle to A-B, centered on X. Mark its ends C and D. Use the protractor to make sure that the angles ACD and ADC are each 60 degrees.

3. Measure 1¾ inches (4.5 cm) back from B along your line A-B. Mark this point Y. Draw a 1¾-inch (4.5-cm) line at a right angle to A-B, centered on Y. Mark its ends E and F. Use the protractor to make sure that the angles BEF and BFE are each 60 degrees.

4. Use the ruler to find the center point Z on your line A-B. With the drawing compass, mark a circle 3 inches (7.5 cm) around Z. Use the ruler to draw a 3-inch (7.5-cm) square around the circle. Mark its corners G, H, I, and J.

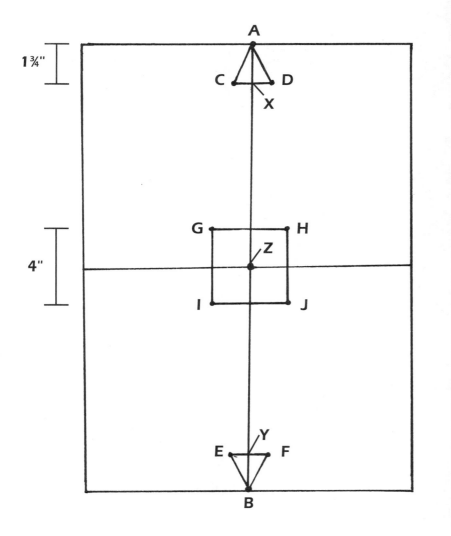

PAPYRUS

Papyrus is a reed that grows in the Nile Delta and other warm, moist places. It is a big, leafy plant with a thick stem that grows taller than a person. The ancient Egyptians made all kinds of things from papyrus. They sliced the stems in thin strips and laid them on top of each other in a crisscross pattern. Then they beat the papyrus so it blended together and became a sheet that they could write on. This was the earliest paper, and our word **paper** comes from **papyrus.** The Egyptians also made sandals from papyrus. They even made boats from it, as well as sails for the boats.

5. Rule lines G-C, H-D, I-E, and J-F. Cut out the whole illustration as a single piece; do not cut it up into small pieces!

6. Put half your obelisk on the poster board, and trace around it as shown below. Use the ruler and pencil to draw a tab ½ inch (1.25 cm) around each side. (You will use these tabs to glue the obelisk together.) Cut out around the tabs.

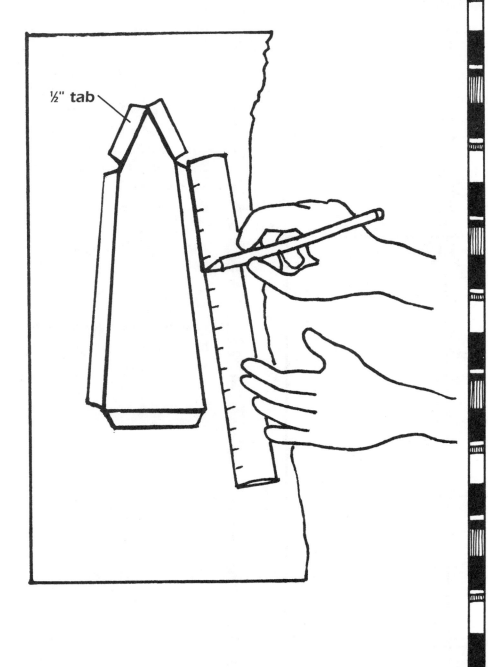

½" tab

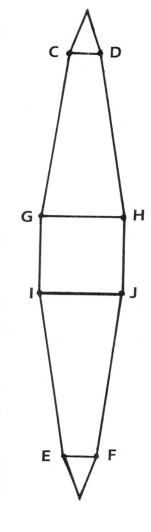

7. Repeat step 6 with the other half.

8. Decorate your obelisk. Choose a hieroglyphic message from the previous activity. Remember to put all names inside a cartouche! Draw your hieroglyphs in pencil from top to bottom down the sides of your obelisk. Use the markers to go over your signs.

9. Assemble your obelisk. Fold up the two sides around the base, G-H-E-F. Bend a fold along the triangle lines C-D and E-F. Bend a fold along the tab lines from steps 6 and 7. Put a thin line of glue along the tabs, then press your obelisk together.

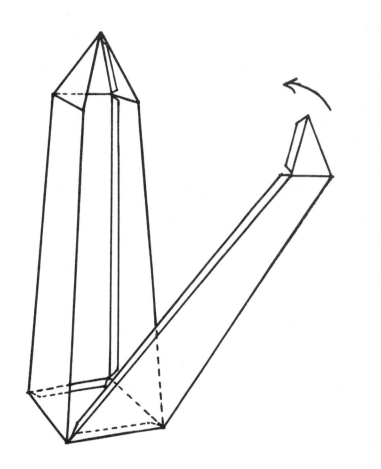

OBELISKS

The ancient Egyptians raised tall stone columns in honor of the sun god Re. These were usually carved from one huge block of granite, as tall as 97 feet (29 m). They were often put in pairs on each side of a temple's doors. The obelisk's top was shaped like a pyramid. Down each side the names and titles of the pharaoh were carved in hieroglyphs. Obelisks can be seen in Egypt at Heliopolis and Karnak. Several Egyptian obelisks were moved to other countries in the eighteenth and nineteenth centuries. In both New York and London you can see an obelisk called Cleopatra's Needle. Paris and Rome also have Egyptian obelisks.

CHAPTER·5

A CAT'S JOURNEY TO THE AFTERLIFE

Paneb and Ipy walk home quickly from the pyramid site. They need to join Neferure, Meryt, Tutu, and Pashed at the funeral ceremony for their older cat Nakht, who recently died.

The family gathers in the house's entryway, near the statue of Bes. Pashed brings a bowl of water and a sharp knife and sets a stool out in the bright sunlight. Pashed regularly shaves Paneb's beard, but today he is going to shave off the eyebrows of everyone in the family, out of respect for the dead cat. Meryt and Ipy are a little nervous, but Pashed is a good barber and whisks off their eyebrows quickly and neatly.

As they look out along the street, Meryt and Ipy see an important-looking man walking toward their house. This is Sennefer, who is a priest and an *embalmer*, a craftsman who prepares a dead body for its everlasting life. Sennefer wears a jackal mask in honor of Anubis, the god of the underworld.

When Sennefer comes in, Neferure bows and leads him into the dining room where Nakht's body is laid on a table. Sennefer leads them in prayers to Bastet. Then his servant opens his box of tools, and he starts to make the cat mummy. First he removes its brain, which he discards. He then removes the liver, spleen, intestines, and lungs, and places them in clay pots called *canopic jars.* He fills the cat's body with herbs and spices, sews it up, and covers it with *natron*, a salt that preserves it. Then he wraps it in linen, with more spices. When he is finished, he paints a cat's face on the linen wrapping, so it looks lifelike. Then he puts the cat mummy inside a hollow, life-size bronze statue of a cat, which he has brought with him.

CATS IN EGYPT

Egyptians kept many kinds of animals as pets, but they were especially fond of cats. Egyptians regarded cats as faithful friends and adorned them with gold earrings, necklaces, and amulets. They valued cats for protecting their stores of grain from mice and rats, and for their help in hunting birds. Egyptians also honored cats because they represented the goddess Bastet, who was the goddess of happiness and love. When an Egyptian cat died, the family who owned the cat mourned it. Dead cats were mummified like people, and thousands of cats were buried in a cemetery at Bastet's temple at Bubastis, near Giza.

ACTIVITY

APPLE MUMMY

The Egyptians were able to preserve bodies by drying them out.
We call these preserved bodies mummies, a word that comes
from *mummiya,* the Arabic word for bitumen. People thought
that the Egyptians used bitumen to make mummies, but the
Egyptians actually used regular table salt or natron, another salt
found in the Delta at a dried lakebed called Wadi Natrun. You
can make natron by mixing table salt and baking soda. In this
activity you can make an apple into a mummy by using table salt
or natron.

MATERIALS

2 apples, cut in half
plate
1 pound (0.5 kg) of table salt
¼ pound (125 gm) of baking soda, mixed with the salt (optional)
plastic box, big enough to hold 1 apple

1. Put one apple out on a plate.

2. Pour an inch of salt (either table salt or the salt and
baking soda mix) in the box. Put the other apple in
the salt and press the two halves down until the salt
covers as much as possible. Pour more salt in until
both halves of the apple are completely covered.

3. Keep both apples on a shelf for two weeks.

4. Compare the two apples.

5. Wait four weeks and six
weeks, and compare the two
apples again. What has the salt
done to the apple in the box?

ACTIVITY
SARCOPHAGUS

A human mummy was usually put inside a coffin called a **sarcophagus,** on which were painted special designs to keep the spirit happy. The coffin had to have a magic door to allow the ba to fly out at night, and eyes to allow the spirit to look out from his coffin. Decorate this Egyptian coffin with traditional designs.

MATERIALS

several sheets of newspaper
shoe box
five 9-by-12-inch (23-by-30-cm) sheets of white construction paper
pencil
ruler
scissors
white glue
black marker
paints in several colors
paintbrush
water jar

1. Spread the newspaper over your work surface.

2. Trace each surface of the box on the white paper. Cut the pieces out, and glue them to the box.

3. Wait for all the glue to dry.

4. Now decorate your box with the designs shown here.

THE BOOK OF THE DEAD

We know about Egyptian funeral rituals from **The Book of the Dead.** This was a book that told what would happen to the spirit after death. This book was buried with the dead, so they could refer to it. It told how their heart would be weighed against the feather of Ma'at, goddess of truth. If they had done wicked things when they were alive, they would be judged unfit to live in the happy afterlife.

ACTIVITY

MUMMY FIGURE

To prepare the body for its eternal life, the Egyptians dried it and wrapped it in linen and spices, with amulets to keep it safe. In this activity you can make a mummy shape and paint it with designs like an Egyptian mummy.

MATERIALS

sarcophagus from previous activity
cubit stick from activity on pages 20-21 (or any ruler)
9 single sheets of newspaper
scissors
masking tape
bowl of water
2 cups (0.5 l) of wallpaper paste
water
paper towels
poster paint or acrylic paint
brush
water jar

1. Take the sarcophagus you made in the previous activity and measure its length with your cubit stick or ruler. You need to make your mummy about 1 inch (2.5 cm) shorter than the sarcophagus.

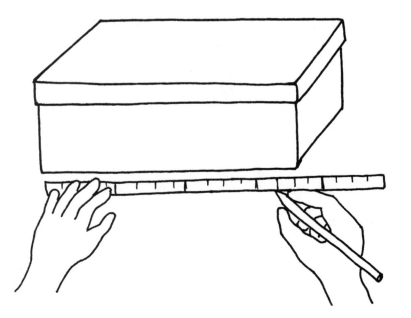

2. Spread three sheets of newspaper over your work area. Tear the other sheets of newspaper in half, to make twelve pages.

3. Take one sheet of torn newspaper and fold the top half down. Make sure that the folded paper measures about 1 inch (2.5 cm) less than your mummy case. If necessary, cut off a strip of newspaper.

4. Roll up the folded newspaper tightly. Tape it with a piece of masking tape.

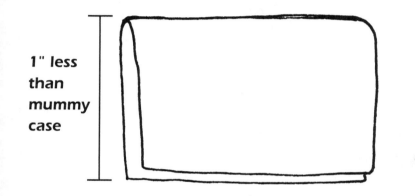

1" less than mummy case

MUMMY MEDICINE

If you lived 150 years ago, you might have been given a spoonful of mummy to take when you felt sick! After mummies were discovered in Egypt, many people in Europe and America believed that they had great healing powers. They ground the mummy up into powder and gave it as medicine for all kinds of diseases!

5. Take a second page of newspaper, fold it, and wrap it around the first roll. Tape it together. Cut it down if necessary so that it still fits in the mummy case.

6. Continue with the other ten pages of newspaper, rolling and wrapping them tightly. The finished roll should measure about 3 inches (7.5 cm) around. Use plenty of masking tape to hold it firmly.

7. Measure 3 inches (7.5 cm) down from one end of the roll. Pinch in the paper to make the neck. Wrap masking tape around it to hold it in.

8. Make the top of the head round by pushing on it, and tape it down to hold the round shape.

9. Squeeze the other end of the mummy to make it narrower, and fold the bottom edge out to make the feet. Tape the feet to hold them in place.

10. Make papier-mâché: Put the paste in a bowl. Tear up four sheets of newspaper in strips. Dip them in the wallpaper paste to wet them through.

11. Shake each strip to remove excess paste. Take a strip and wrap it around the mummy to make a smooth cover. Continue until all the strips are used and the mummy is covered. Let the mummy dry overnight.

12. Draw an oval over the face. Paint the face with black outline around the eyes and features. Paint the rest of your mummy with Egyptian designs as shown in the illustration.

ACTIVITY
CAT STATUE

The Egyptians made many beautiful life-size statues of cats. Some of them were made hollow, so that a cat mummy could be put inside. The cat is often shown wearing gold earrings or a necklace with an amulet.

MATERIALS

newspaper
self-hardening clay, 1½ pounds (0.75 kg)
resealable plastic bag
paper clip
pen
pair of earrings (optional)

1. Spread the newspaper over your work surface.

2. Squeeze the clay in your hands until it feels warm. Divide the clay into four balls. The biggest ball should be the size of a large orange. The next two balls should be the same size, like a golf ball. The smallest ball should be the size of a large marble. Keep out the biggest ball. Put the three other balls into the plastic bag and seal it.

3. Make the cat's body by shaping the largest ball into an egg shape. Flatten one pointed end of the egg to be the bottom. Place it on the table and be sure it stands up.

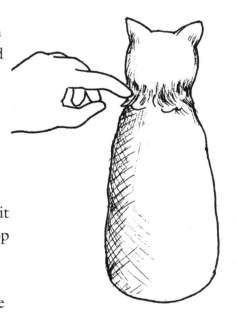

4. Make the cat's head. Take one of the golf-ball-size pieces of clay out of the bag and roll it into a ball. Place the ball on top of the body and blend the clay up from the body into the head. Push down gently on the head.

THE BA

The Egyptians believed that each person's soul has several different parts. One part was the ba, or the individual personality. This spirit had the head of the dead person but the body of a bird. By day the ba stayed in his tomb, but at night he could fly out and visit his home and other places he enjoyed when he was alive. The ba needed food, so meals were painted on tomb walls, model food was placed inside the tomb, and real food offerings were brought to the tomb for him.

5. Take the other golf-ball-size piece of clay and divide it into three equal parts. Roll each of the three parts into a long, thick rope.

6. Take two of the clay ropes and shape them into the front legs and paws. Attach them at the shoulders, under the head. Smooth the clay where the legs join the body.

7. Take the third rope and shape it into the tail. Attach one end to the center back of the cat. Wrap it around the right side of the cat to meet the right front paw.

8. Take the smallest ball of clay and divide it in two. Take one of the small pieces and shape it into a back paw. Attach it to the lower left side of the cat, just behind the left front paw.

9. Take the other small piece of clay and shape it into a nose. Push it onto the face. Smooth the clay where the nose joins the body.

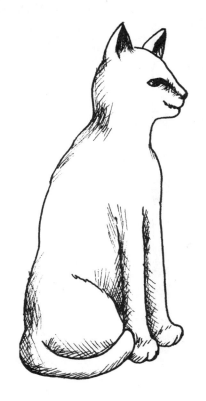

10. Take the paper clip and open up one end. Use the point to make a hole in each ear. Make it big enough for an earring to fit.

11. Let the clay dry for two days, away from heat. When it is dry, use the pen to draw eyes on the face. Then draw a necklace and amulet hanging around the cat's neck, for luck. Ask your mom if you can borrow a pair of earrings to hang in its ears.

THE KA

Another part of the spirit was the ka, the life force that lived in every person. When someone died, the ka separated from the body but went on living. The ka looked exactly the same as the dead person had when he was alive. A statue of the dead person was placed in his tomb to guide the ka back to his body. The ka statue had a special symbol, a pair of arms with upraised hands placed on top of the statue's head to keep evil away. Like the ba, the ka needed food in his tomb.

CHAPTER·6

A HUNT IN THE DELTA

After their cat's mummy is finished, the family prepares to go hunting in the Delta, where Nakht used to love to go. They hope to catch some birds for this evening's dinner. Meryt gets their young cat, Ani, and carries her along.

Neferure and Tutu finish packing their lunch, and everyone sets out on the raised path through the fields to the Nile. Paneb carries spears and sticks for the hunt. Pashed walks behind Paneb and Neferure, waving a palm-leaf fan to cool them and keep the flies away. Tutu brings two reed baskets. There are pitchers of beer in one basket and bread, dates, and figs in the other. Meryt has another basket with pottery cups and linen napkins, and a game called Serpent. Ipy carries their boat's sail, made from papyrus.

Their boat is stored on the dock, near the harbor. It is made from bundles of papyrus tied together. Ipy helps Pashed and Paneb pick it up and carry it to the water. It is small and light, and good for the shallow waters of the Delta. They set out northward, with Paneb steering. Ipy hangs over the side with a line to catch fish. Meryt sits in the back, holding Ani. The cat becomes excited as they turn out of the main river and into a reedy stream, with all its animal noises. Crocodiles, hippopotamuses, and lions live in the Delta, along with many smaller animals and hundreds of kinds of birds.

When they reach the Delta they want to move slowly, so they let the boat drift, with Pashed using the rudder to steer. Paneb and Ipy hold curved throwing sticks, which they aim at the game. They have spears ready in case a hippopotamus or a crocodile should come too close and threaten to overturn their light boat. Meryt lets Ani out of the boat and onto the bank. The cat joins in the hunt by chasing birds out of the reeds for the hunters. Meryt lets out a line in hopes of catching a fish.

THE NILE: HIGHWAY OF EGYPT

The Nile was the main highway of Egypt, since roads were few and frequently washed away by the flooding river. In the Old Kingdom, when our story takes place, the Egyptians had not yet tamed horses or camels, and they had no carts with wheels. They traveled by walking or by boat. The pharaoh and other important people were carried about on thrones.

On the Nile, boats used both sails and oars to travel up and down the river. The Nile flows from south to north, but the wind on the Nile usually blows from the north. Boats traveling south used their sails, but to move in the other direction, like the barge coming from Aswan to Giza, took hard work by the rowers. The hieroglyph for north is a boat with its sail folded, while the hieroglyph for south is a boat with its sail up.

BOAT

Boats were important in the lives of all Egyptians. When important people were buried, model boats were placed in their tombs so their spirits could go sailing. In this activity you can make a model boat like one placed in a tomb. Egyptian model boats had bigger rudders than a real boat would—perhaps this was to make sure that the soul could steer the boat easily!

MATERIALS

several sheets of newspaper
½ pound (0.25 kg) of self-hardening clay (about the size of an orange)
ruler
pencil
4-by-4-inch (10-by-10-cm) piece of white or tan paper
scissors
4 drinking straws
plastic tape
3-by-2-inch (7.5-by-5-cm) piece of poster board
brown paint
paintbrush and water jar
28-inch (70-cm) piece of red yarn
white glue

1. Spread the newspaper over your work area.

2. Work the clay in your hands until it is soft and warm. Mold the piece of clay into the boat shape shown here. Use the ruler to measure your boat—make it 6½ inches (16.5 cm) long.

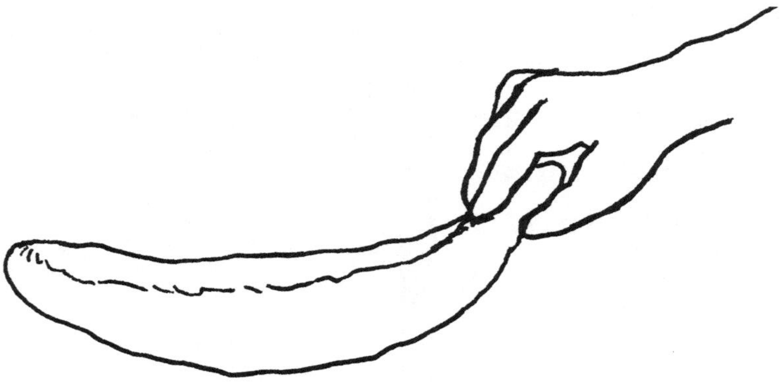

3. Use the pencil and ruler to draw the sail on the paper. Make it a trapezoid, 4 inches (10 cm) wide at the bottom, 4 inches (10 cm) high, and 3 inches (7.5 cm) wide at the top. Cut out the sail. (Save the rest of the paper.)

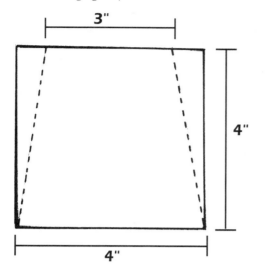

4. Cut one straw 6½ inches (16.5 cm) tall, to be the mast. From another straw, cut a 4-inch (10-cm)-long piece to be the crossbar at the bottom of the sail, and a 3-inch (7.5-cm)-long piece to be the crossbar at the top of the sail.

5. Use the ruler to find the center of each crossbar. Draw a line around the center. Carefully cut two ¼-inch (0.6-cm) notches at the line, one on each side of the straw. Do not cut the straw in half!

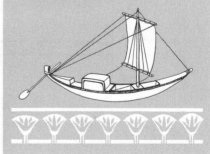

6. Push the crossbars over the mast. Place the 3-inch (7.5-cm) crossbar 1 inch (2.5 cm) from the top. Place the 4-inch (10-cm) crossbar 5 inches (12.5 cm) from the top. Tape the sail to the crossbars.

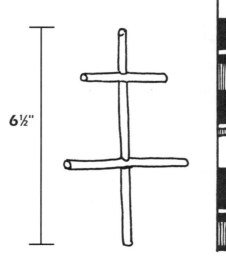

NILE BOATS

To travel to other cities along the Nile, Egyptian families needed a boat. But wood was scarce and expensive in Egypt, where very few large trees grow, so most people owned a small boat made from papyrus reeds. Larger boats were made from wood. The biggest boats of all, like the royal barges in which the pharaoh and the queen traveled or the barges that brought stone to the pyramid site, were built from tall cedars imported from Lebanon. Cheops's royal barge was buried near his tomb. The barge is made from cedar planks and is 150 feet (45 m) long. All boats had sails made from papyrus. Sailboats made from papyrus still sail on the Nile today. They are called *feluccas.*

7. Use the ruler to find the center of the boat. Mark the center point. Place the mast in the boat at the center point. Push the mast ½ inch (1.25 cm) into the clay so that it stands up.

8. On the paper, draw the 1-by-½-inch (2.5-by-1.25-cm) rudder paddle shown here. Cut out the paddle. Take the last straw, and cut a 3-inch (7.5-cm) piece from its end to be the board to hold the rudder. The rest of the straw is the rudder. Cut a ½-inch (1.25-cm) slit at its end. Push the paddle into this slit. Cut two ¼-inch (0.6-cm) notches at the other end of the rudder. Be careful not to cut off the end of the straw!

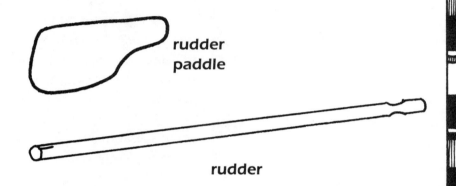

rudder paddle

rudder

9. Push the rudder board through the notches in the rudder. Measure 2 inches (5 cm) from one end of the boat, and mark that spot. At the mark, push the board ½ inch (1.25 cm) into the boat so that it stands.

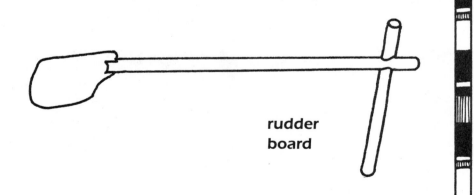

rudder board

10. Copy the drawing of the cabin on your poster board. Cut it out. Bend the sides of the cabin along the lines A-B and C-D. Press the cabin into the boat between the mast and the rudder.

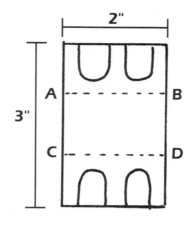

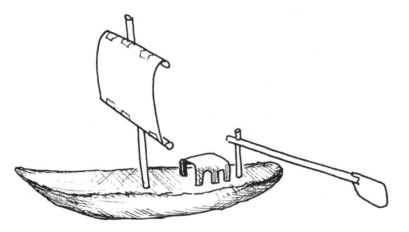

11. Let the clay boat dry for two days, away from sunny windows or heaters. When it is dry, paint your boat brown.

12. When the paint has dried, squeeze a thin line of glue along the sides of the boat. Stick the yarn along the glue so it wraps around the boat.

ACTIVITY

HIPPOPOTAMUS STATUE

Many hippos lived in the warm, shallow rivers of the Delta. The Egyptians were afraid of the hippos because the hippos could easily overturn their light papyrus boats. Statues of hippos are found in tombs, decorated with designs of papyrus reeds on their bodies. The Egyptians made their hippo statues from *faience*, a kind of pottery that has a shiny glaze. The Egyptians usually tinted the glaze blue or blue-green.

TAWERET

Taweret, the hippopotamus goddess, was one of the most popular goddesses in Egypt. She looked after mothers and babies. Like Bes, Taweret had no temples, but her statue was found in almost every home. Taweret was shown as a hippo with human arms and a lion's legs. Like all important Egyptians, she wore a wig. But Taweret's wig ended in a crocodile's tail!

MATERIALS

newspaper
self-hardening clay, 1½ pounds (0.75 kg)
resealable plastic bag
pen
blue or blue-green paint
paintbrush and water jar
black marker

1. Spread the newspaper over your work surface.

2. Squeeze the clay in your hands until it feels warm. Divide the clay into four balls. The biggest ball should be the size of a large orange. The other three balls should each be about the size of a golf ball. Keep out the biggest ball. Put the three other balls into the plastic bag, and seal it.

3. Make the hippo's body by shaping the largest ball into an egg shape. Flatten one rounded end of the egg to be the bottom so it can stand. Place it on the table.

4. Take one of the small pieces of clay out of the bag, and roll it into a ball. This will be the hippo's head. Place the ball on top of the body, and blend the clay up from the body into the head. Push down gently on the head.

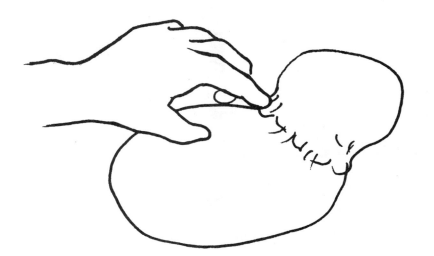

5. Take another small piece of clay, and roll it into a snake shape. Divide the snake into two equal parts. These will be the front legs. Push them gently under the front of the body.

6. Take the last small piece of clay, and roll it into a snake shape. Divide the snake into two equal parts. These will be the back legs. Push them gently under the back of the body. Smooth the clay where all the legs join the body.

7. Use the pen to scratch reeds and flowers along the sides of the hippo. Make him look as if you were looking at him through the reeds of the Delta!

8. Let the clay hippo dry for two days, away from sunny windows or heaters.

9. Paint your hippo blue or blue-green. When the paint is dry, use a black marker to go over the lines of reeds you drew.

By midafternoon it is hot, and the family appreciates the shade of the tall papyrus and other reeds and the breeze off the water as they glide along. Tutu waves their fan to keep insects away. Neferure unpacks their lunch and pours the beer. It is cool and sweet. Beer is the favorite drink of Egyptians. They make it at home, from barley sweetened with dates. They all enjoy their lunch of bread and fruit. After lunch Meryt brings out their game of Serpent, and she and Ipy play.

ACTIVITY

SERPENT GAME

We know about many different games that the Egyptians enjoyed because they placed games and toys in the tombs of important people. Egyptians of all ages enjoyed playing! Serpent was a popular game, consisting of a board made like a snake's body and pieces that the players moved around the snake, trying to be first to reach its head.

MATERIALS

newspaper
self-hardening clay, 1 pound (0.5 kg)
resealable plastic bag
pencil
4 craft sticks
black and red markers
paint
paintbrush and water jar

1. Spread the newspaper over your work surface.

2. Squeeze the clay in your hands until it feels warm. Divide the clay in thirds. Keep two thirds out, and put the rest into the plastic bag and seal it.

3. Make the snake's body by rolling the clay you have kept out into a snake shape. Choose one end of your snake to be the head. Hold it 2 inches (5 cm) above your work area, and twist the rest of the snake in a spiral on your table to be the body.

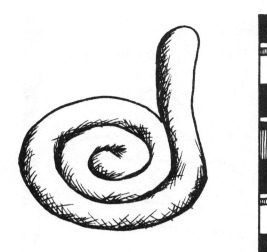

4. Press the head so its top is flat. Smooth all the clay. Use the pencil to mark a line dividing the snake's body into sections 1 inch (2.5 cm) wide. Mark four lucky and four unlucky sections on the board, as shown in the picture. With the pencil, draw the hieroglyph for "river" on the lucky squares and the hieroglyph for "desert" on the unlucky squares.

river   **desert**

5. Take the other third of the clay out of the plastic bag. Divide it into fourths. Shape each piece into a cone with a flat bottom so it will stand. These are the playing pieces.

6. Take the craft sticks and draw one of the hieroglyphs shown here on one side of each craft stick. These are the throw sticks.

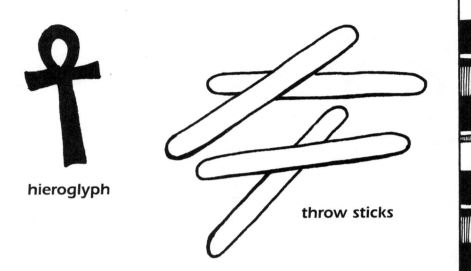

hieroglyph

throw sticks

7. Let the snake and playing pieces dry for two days, away from sunny windows or heaters. When they are dry, paint your snake blue or blue-green, and paint each of the playing pieces a different color. Use the black marker to go over the lucky hieroglyphs on the snake's body, and the red marker to go over the unlucky hieroglyphs.

HOW TO PLAY SERPENT

Two to four players can play. Each player has a playing piece, and the object is to be the first player to move your playing piece around the board and up to the snake's head.

To start, each player takes a turn throwing all four throwing sticks up in the air. When they land, count how many of the hieroglyphs you can see. Whoever gets the most hieroglyphs at the first throw starts the game. The first player puts his playing piece on the first section of the snake's tail and throws the sticks, then moves his playing piece the number of hieroglyphs showing. The other players follow in turn. There are four lucky squares, marked in black by the hieroglyph for river. If a player lands on a lucky square, he moves ahead by twice the number he has thrown. There are four unlucky squares, marked in red by the hieroglyph for desert. If a player lands on an unlucky square, he falls back by twice the number he has thrown. The first player to reach the head of the snake is the winner.

CHAPTER 7

GETTING READY FOR THE FESTIVAL

The hunt is a success! The family has caught a fine fat goose and four small birds! Their feast will be a good one, worthy of the goddess Bastet. They come home happy but tired, and they rest on the roof for an hour as the sun begins to move lower in the sky.

Neferure is the first to get up. She and Tutu have to get everything ready for the evening celebration. First they prepare baths for the family. Tutu and Pashed go to the village cistern to get jugs of water. They bring the water to the bathroom, which has a stone slab on the floor.

Each member of the family in turn stands on the slab while the servants pour water over them. They rub perfume on their skin and dry themselves with linen towels.

Next, the adults paint cosmetics on their faces. Like all Egyptians who can afford it, Neferure and Paneb wear wigs on special occasions. Neferure takes out the reed baskets in which the family's wigs are kept. Meryt watches carefully as her mother combs and curls the hair. They tie cones of perfumed wax on top of their wigs. In the heat, the wax melts and runs down their hair, scenting them. Last of all they put on their pleated festival gowns and kilts, their jewelry and headdresses.

ACTIVITY

FACE PAINTING

Both men and women in Egypt outlined their eyes with a black powder called *kohl,* and they colored their lips and cheeks red. Sometimes they painted some green around their eyes, too. They mixed the cosmetic powders on a palette, a small tray often shaped like an animal. These palettes were buried with important people, along with small boxes to hold the powder. In this activity, see how you look when your face is painted like an ancient Egyptian!

MATERIALS

Egyptian eye makeup picture
nontoxic face paint in red, green, and black
3 small brushes or cotton swabs
jar of water
tissues
mirror
adult helper

1. Ask your adult helper to study the Egyptian eye makeup picture here and to outline your eyes and eyebrows with a black line. Note how the line around the eyes and eyebrows extends back over the cheekbones. Be careful not to get any paint in your eyes. If you do, immediately wash it out with water.

2. Have your helper add a green line outside the black line.

3. Using the mirror, paint your lips red.

ACTIVITY

PERFUME CONE

In this activity you can make a perfume cone that is sure not to melt!

MATERIALS

3-inch (7.5-cm) diameter Styrofoam or sponge ball
sharp knife
scissors
white cloth 9 inches (23 cm) square, such as an old handkerchief

EGYPTIAN ART

Egyptian art was made for religious reasons, not just to be enjoyed. Much great art was made for tombs of kings and queens, so most people would never see it. Egyptian paintings of people are easy to recognize. The heads and feet are shown from the side, while the arms and bodies are shown from the front. Very often the people are shown honoring a god. The god usually has an animal head on a human body or is made up of several different animals. There is usually hieroglyphic writing painted inside the picture, or in a border around it.

3 feet (90 cm) of narrow ribbon
duct tape
perfume
adult helper

1. Ask your adult helper to cut the ball in half. Discard one half.

2. Wrap the cloth over the half ball. Use duct tape to stick the cloth to the bottom of ball.

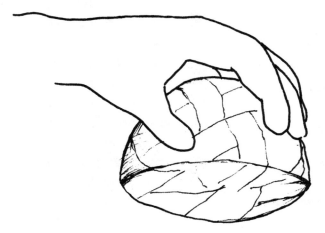

3. Cut the ribbon in half. Use a small piece of duct tape to stick half of the ribbon on the bottom of the ball on opposite sides.

4. Sprinkle a few drops of perfume on top of the ball.

5. Put the ball on top of your head. Tie the ribbons under your hair or under your chin. Now enjoy your perfume cone!

ACTIVITY

BROAD COLLAR

One of the most typical pieces of Egyptian jewelry was the broad collar worn by both men and women. It was made of rows of gold beads, gems, and decorated faience. Make yourself a colorful collar in this activity! You can vary the colors if you wish.

MATERIALS

ruler
colored pencil
sheet of newspaper
drawing compass
scissors
4 pieces of felt, each 1 square foot (30 square cm), in white, blue,
  red, and green
straight pins
3-by-5-inch (7-by-12-cm) index card
fabric glue
safety pin (optional)
gold or other colored braid

1. Make a paper pattern for your collar. Use the colored pencil and ruler to measure a 12-inch (30-cm) square on the newspaper. Draw two diagonal lines from corner to corner of the square. They will cross at the center point.

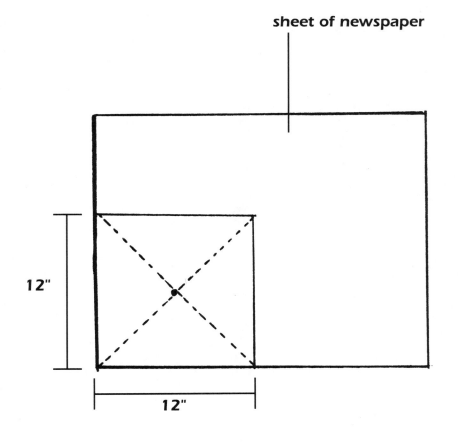

sheet of newspaper

12"

12"

PERFUME CONE

Egyptian art often shows men and women in Egypt sitting at feasts with a cone on top of their heads. Historians believe that this was a perfume cone made of scented fat that would have melted in the heat of the party and released a scent.

2. Put the drawing compass and colored pencil at the center point, and draw a circle 4 inches (10 cm) in diameter. Draw another circle 6 inches (15 cm) in diameter. Draw another circle 8 inches (20 cm) in diameter. Draw another circle 10 inches (25 cm) in diameter. Draw another circle 12 inches (30 cm) in diameter. Cut out your pattern around the largest circle.

3. Pin the pattern to the white felt square. Cut out the felt around the pattern, along the largest circle. Make a hole for your neck by starting a cut at the center of the felt and cutting out along the smallest circle.

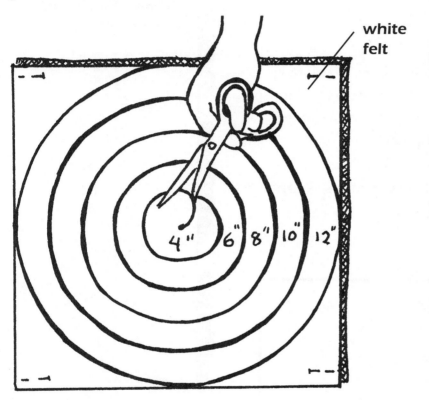

white felt

4. Unpin your paper pattern, and make it smaller by cutting around the 10-inch (25-cm) circle. Discard the strip of paper you have cut off. Pin the pattern to the green felt square. Cut out the felt around the pattern, making a 10-inch (25-cm) circle.

5. Unpin your pattern, and make it smaller by cutting around the 8-inch (20-cm) circle. Discard the strip of paper you have cut off. Pin the pattern back onto the green circle. Cut around the 8-inch (20-cm) circle to make a 2-inch (5-cm)-wide green ring.

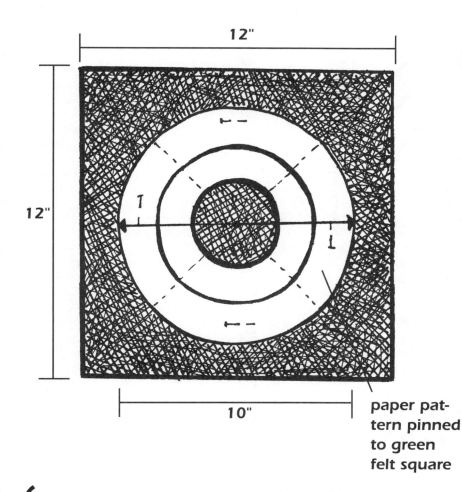

12"

12"

10"

paper pattern pinned to green felt square

6. Unpin the pattern, and pin it to the red felt square. Cut out the felt around the pattern, making an 8-inch (20-cm) circle. Unpin your pattern, and make it smaller by cutting around the 6-inch (15-cm) circle. Discard the strip of paper you have cut off. Pin the pattern back onto the red felt circle. Cut around the 6-inch (15-cm) circle to make a 2-inch (5-cm)-wide red ring.

7. Unpin the pattern, and pin it to the blue felt square. Cut out the felt around the pattern, making a 6-inch (15-cm) circle. Unpin the pattern, and make it smaller by cutting around the 4-inch (10-cm) circle. Pin the pattern back onto the blue felt circle. Cut around the 4-inch (10-cm) circle to make a 2-inch (5-cm)-wide blue ring.

8. To assemble the collar, squeeze a thin line of glue all along the edges of the blue felt circle. Press it around the neck hole of the white felt circle. Then squeeze a thin line of glue all along the edges of the red felt circle. Press it onto the white felt circle, outside the blue ring. Then squeeze a thin line of glue all along the edges of the green felt circle. Press it onto the white felt circle, outside the red ring.

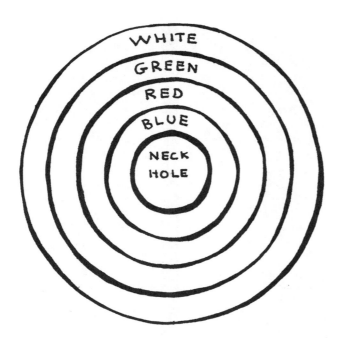

9. Decorate the outer circle. Copy the papyrus and lotus shapes drawn here onto the card with the colored pencil. Cut them out. Take the scraps of blue, green, and red felt. On each color felt, trace three papyrus and three lotus patterns. Cut them out, and glue them onto the white felt ring.

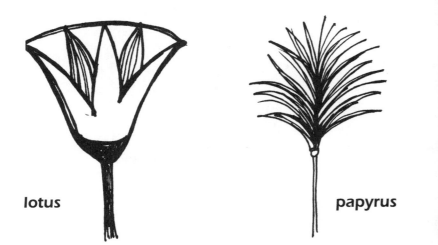

lotus   papyrus

10. If your head doesn't fit comfortably inside your collar, cut a slit through the back of the collar. Fasten the collar with a safety pin. If you like, glue some gold or other colored braid onto the blue and green rings of your collar.

ACTIVITY

ARMLET

Egyptian men and women wore wide gold bands on their upper arms and wrists and even on their ankles. Sometimes these were decorated with pictures in faience and sometimes with colorful gems.

MATERIALS

thin cardboard 3 by 12 inches (7.5 by 30 cm)
scissors
duct tape
florist's gold foil or aluminum foil 5 by 12 inches (12.5 by 30 cm)
colored glass "gems" with one flat side, from a craft store
white glue
2 strips of 12-inch (30-cm) colored braid

1. Wrap the cardboard around your upper arm. Cut off the excess. Fasten the ends together with duct tape.

2. Wrap the armlet in foil.

3. Glue the colored braid around the edges of the armlet. Glue the "gems" onto the armlet.

EGYPTIAN JEWELS

Ancient Egyptians loved to wear gold jewelry and to include gems in household furnishings and religious objects. The Egyptians had no emeralds, rubies, or diamonds, but they had many other colorful stones. Blue lapis lazuli and red carnelian were two of their most popular stones, along with blue-green turquoise. Green faience was also used for jewelry and decoration. Tombs contain a great deal of jewelry that was buried with the dead for them to enjoy in the afterlife.

CHAPTER 8

CELEBRATION AT THE TEMPLE OF BASTET

Once she is all dressed up, Meryt goes to the living room to get her sistrum and menat. She needs them to play at the temple ceremonies this afternoon. The whole family is coming to the temple of the cat goddess Bastet in Bubastis, to celebrate the pharaoh's jubilee. Priests and other people are gathering from far and near to honor the pharaoh at the temple of one of their most beloved goddesses. The family will present the mummy of their old cat Nakht to Bastet. Nakht will then be buried near the temple in a cemetery for cats.

Ipy and Pashed walk down to the dock. They have left

their boat on the edge of the water, ready to sail again. Neferure carries the cat mummy and puts it carefully in the middle of the boat. Then they set out for Bubastis, a short distance away.

As they get near to Bubastis, they can all hear music and the noise of the crowds who are arriving for the festival. Meryt begins to feel nervous. There will be a big procession around the temple, with hundreds of people taking part. Meryt had forgotten how many people would be there to hear her play!

They all walk up to the temple doorway. Huge pylons guard the door, and two tall obelisks reflect the sunlight from their copper pyramid tops. Inside the temple the priests and priestesses are praying and offering sacrifices to Bastet. Neferure gives the mummy of Nakht to a priestess, who carries it inside the temple to dedicate it to Bastet before its burial.

BASTET

Bastet was a powerful Egyptian goddess associated with happiness, and protector of all the cats kept as pets in Egypt. She was shown as a cat, or as a woman with the head of a cat. Thousands of mummified cats were buried near her temple at Bubastis in the Delta, and a popular festival was held there in her honor every year.

ACTIVITY

HORN AND SUN DISK HEADDRESS

Make your own Hathor headdress, and wear it when you are feeling cheerful.

MATERIALS

blue poster board 28 by 11 inches (71 by 27.5 cm)
ruler
pencil
drawing compass
scissors
black marker
6½-inch (16.25-cm) square of florist's gold foil or aluminum foil
glue
duct tape
stapler

1. Use the ruler and pencil to draw a strip along the edge of the poster board 28 inches (71 cm) long by 1¼ inches (3 cm) wide. Mark the center point of the strip.

2. Line up the edge of the ruler with the center point on the strip. Measure up 5 inches (12.5 cm) from the center point to point A. Put the drawing compass on A, and draw a circle with a radius of 3¼ inches (8 cm). Draw two lines 1¼ inches (3 cm) apart, connecting the circle and the long strip.

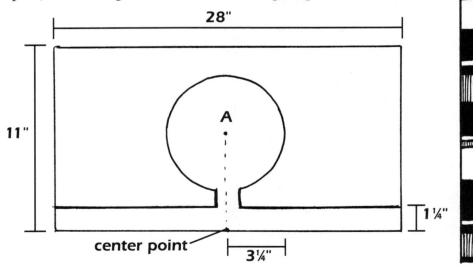

3. Copy the drawing of the horns shown below around the circle. The tips of the horns should be 11 inches (27.5 cm) high and 16 inches (41 cm) apart.

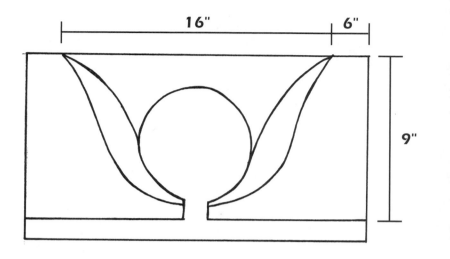

HATHOR

Hathor was one of the most popular Egyptian goddesses. She was the daughter of the great sun god Re and was the goddess of young people, love, beauty, and music. She was often shown as a cow, or sometimes as a woman wearing a headdress of the sun, her father, inside a cow's horns.

4. Cut out your headdress. Save the leftover poster board.

5. Use the drawing compass to draw a circle 3 inches (7.5 cm) in radius on the gold or aluminum foil. Cut out this circle. Put a thin line of glue in a spiral all around the edge and across the center of the foil. Stick it onto the sun disk. Use the black marker to go over the lines around the sun disk and horns.

6. Use the ruler and pencil to measure a rectangle 7 by 5 inches (17.5 by 12.5 cm) on the leftover poster board. Cut this out. Fold this strip in half the long way, and then in half again, to make a 7-by-1¼-inch (17.5-by-3-cm) rectangle.

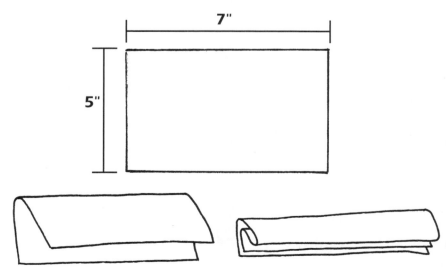

7. Turn the headdress over. Place the folded poster board on the back of the headdress, as shown below. Cut six strips of duct tape 2 inches (5 cm) long. Use the duct tape to stick the strip of poster board onto the back of the headdress to hold it firm.

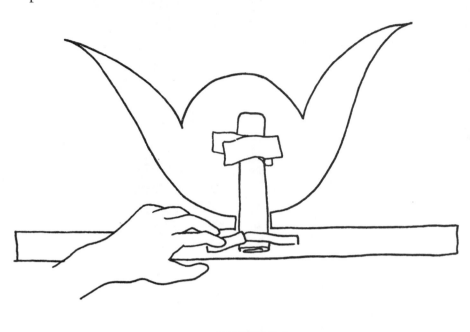

Outside the temple a group of girls with harps and sistra is forming a line on each side of the path where the procession will pass. Meryt joins her friends and takes her place in the line. She will shake the sistrum and menat in time to the song that the priestesses are playing on their harps. Meryt and all the girls will sing, too—they never play without singing, or sing without playing. As soon as she starts to sing, Meryt forgets to be nervous. Ipy feels quite proud as he listens.

Soon a procession of priests and priestesses comes out from the temple. The local priests and priestesses of Bastet lead the way, followed by visiting priests and priestesses from many other temples in the Delta and beyond. There are priests of Osiris from Saqqara, carrying statues of their sacred Apis bull, and priestesses of Hathor from Dendera in Upper Egypt, wearing headdresses with cow horns and a sun disk. Priests of Anubis wear the black jackal mask of their god, and priests of Sobek wear their crocodile masks.

ACTIVITY

JACKAL MASK

Egyptians made many statues and other images of Anubis. Embalmers wore a headdress of a jackal's head in honor of Anubis. Wear your mask, and take part in an Egyptian parade.

MATERIALS
21-by-13-inch (54-by-33-cm) sheet of paper
pencil
ruler
scissors
masking tape
21-by-13-inch (54-by-33-cm) black poster board
stapler
paper punch
one 2-foot (60-cm) piece of string or yarn

1. Make a pattern. Use the pencil and ruler to measure a 21-by-13-inch (54-by-33-cm) rectangle on the paper. Cut this out. Fold the paper in half the long way so it measures 10½ by 13 inches (27 by 33 cm), as shown on page 82. The folded edge of the paper will be the front of the mask.

2. Use the ruler to find the center point of one short side, at 5¾ inches (14.5 cm). Mark this point A, the tip of the ear. Measure down 3½ inches (8.75 cm) from A to B. Measure 1½ inches (3.75 cm) from B in each direction to points B-1 (right) and B-2 (left), the ends of the ears. Rule a line from A to B-1 and A to B-2.

THE APIS BULL

The Egyptians valued all cattle. One particular kind of bull was sacred to Osiris, the god of craftsmen. This was the Apis bull, a living bull who had to be all black, with a triangle of white hair on his forehead. While he was alive, the Apis bull lived in a palace at Saqqara, near Memphis. When he died he was mummified and buried in a great stone tomb, almost like a pharaoh. Many of the Apis bulls were buried together in a big underground tomb at Saqqara, called the Serapeum. The Apis bull is sometimes shown with a sun disk on his head, like the goddess Hathor.

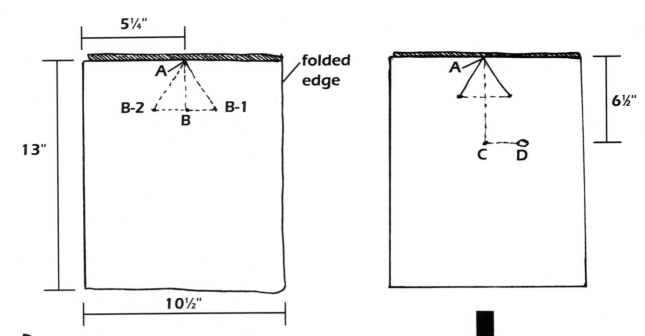

3. Use the ruler to measure down 6½ inches (16.25 cm) from A to C. Measure 1 inch (2.5 cm) to the right of C. Mark this point D. Draw an eye at D.

4. Use the ruler to draw a light line from the eye to the folded edge. Mark this point E, the top of the nose. Draw a line from E up to B-1. Measure down 2½ inches (6.25 cm) from E. This is F, the bottom of the nose. Measure 4 inches (10 cm) to the left from F and mark point G. Draw line F-G.

5. From the lower left corner H, measure up 6 inches (15 cm) to I. Rule a line to join I and B-2. This is the back of the head.

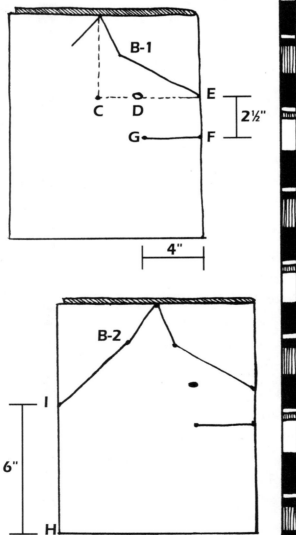

6. From H, measure 3 inches (7.5 cm) to the right to J, the end of the neck. Rule a line from J to G, the front of the neck. Cut out around your pattern. Cut out the eyes.

7. Open up your pattern, and use the masking tape to hold it on the poster board. Cut out around your pattern. Cut out the eyes. Take the pattern off the poster board.

8. Punch a hole between points H and I on each side of the mask. Cut the string in half and tie a piece to the holes you have made. Fold the poster board in half the short way, so that the ears and nose line up. Put three staples along the top of the nose. Try on your mask, and tie the ends of the string behind your head.

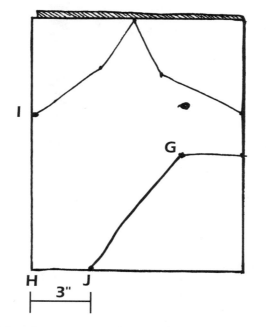

ACTIVITY

CROCODILE MASK

Sobek was the crocodile god of Egypt. He was the patron of a city called Crocodilopolis, where sacred crocodiles were given jewelry to wear and kept in special pools. He was valued because he took care of supplying the water that people needed. Make a mask of Sobek in this activity.

MATERIALS
21-by-11½-inch (53.5-by-28.75-cm) green poster board
ruler

ANUBIS

Anubis was the Egyptian god of the underworld, where people went after they died. He was shown as a jackal, an animal like a dog. He was always black, with big, pointed ears. Anubis was a very important god, since he could make sure that your soul would have a happy life forever.

pencil

black marker

scissors

clear plastic tape

stapler

paper hole punch

2-foot (60-cm) piece of string or yarn

1. Make the top of the mask. Starting at corner A of the poster board, use the ruler and pencil to mark point B 4½ inches (11.25 cm) along the long side. Measure point C 4½ inches (11.25 cm) beyond B. Rule a dotted line from B to point D on the opposite side of the board. Measure 2¼ inches (5.6 cm) on either side of D, and mark these points d-1 and d-2. Rule a line joining d-1 to A, and another line joining d-2 to C. Cut out the trapezoid d-1 to A to C to d-2.

2. Make the base of the mask. Use the ruler and pencil to mark point E 2¾ inches (7 cm) along the long side beyond point C. Measure point F 2¾ inches (7 cm) beyond E. Rule a dotted line from E to point G on the opposite side of the board. Measure 1¼ inches (3 cm) on either side of G, and mark these points g-1 and g-2. Rule a line joining g-1 to C, and another line joining g-2 to F. Cut out the trapezoid g-1 to C to F to g-2.

3. To make the teeth, start at bottom corner Q of your remaining poster board and measure 1¼ inches (3 cm) to q-1. Measure another 1¼ inches (3 cm) from q-1 to q-2. Rule two straight lines across the board joining q-1 to r-1, and q-2 to r-2. Cut out these two long strips. Draw the tooth pattern shown here on each strip, and cut out around the pattern.

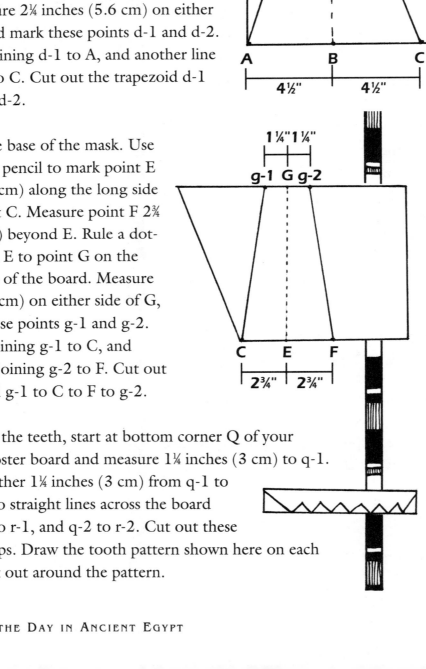
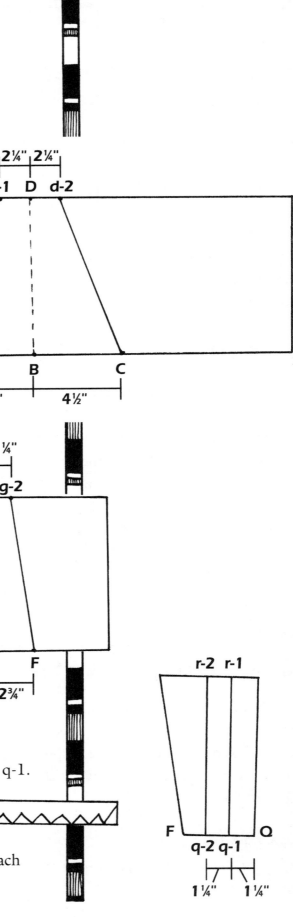

4. Make the snout. Measure a rectangle 3¾ by 2¼ inches (9.5 by 5.6 cm). Cut out the rectangle. Draw the pattern shown here for the snout, and cut it out.

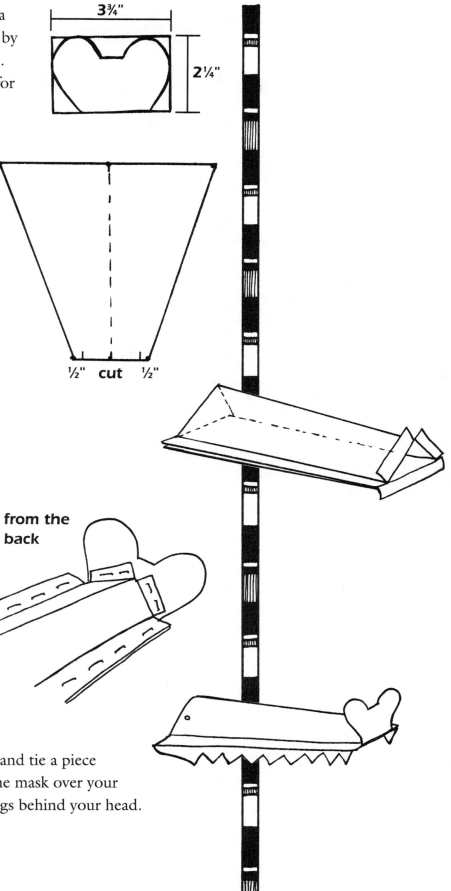

3¾"

2¼"

5. Assemble the mask. Take the top piece. On the narrow end, make a cut ½ inch (1.25 cm) deep and ½ inch (1.25 cm) in from each edge. Fold the top in half the long way. Cut another ½-inch (1.25-cm) slit along the central fold. Make a ½-inch (1.25-cm) fold along the long sides of the top. Place the top on the base. Staple them together along the long edges.

½" **cut** ½"

6. At the narrow end of the top, bend the two outer tabs down and the two inner tabs up. Staple the snout to the inner tabs and to the front of the base. Attach the teeth to the long sides of the base with plastic tape. Bend the teeth down. At the back of the base, punch a hole in the corners. Cut the string in half, and tie a piece through each hole. Now put the mask over your nose and chin, and tie the strings behind your head.

from the back

CHAPTER·9
A ROYAL JUBILEE

After the priestesses have finished their prayers to Bastet, Meryt and the other singers put down their sistra and menats and walk back to their families. Neferure and Paneb congratulate Meryt on her singing and playing. Meryt is happy that her part of the ceremony is over and that it all went well. Now she can really enjoy the pharaoh's jubilee.

Meryt and Ipy sit at the edge of the path leading up to the temple pylons, waiting for the pharaoh to arrive. They have never seen the pharaoh before, so they are very excited.

Soon the high priest gives a signal. Ipy nudges Meryt, and all the people grow very quiet. They turn to face the

Nile, where the pharaoh's boat is pulling in to the dock. Ipy stands tall, and Paneb holds up Meryt so she can see over people's heads. They have never seen such a beautiful boat! It is huge, made of long cedar logs. The pharaoh and the queen are sitting on a raised platform under a canopy, being cooled by servants with elegant palm fans. Rows of oarsmen pull together, as the steersman guides the boat to its mooring.

The pharaoh and queen step out and walk slowly up to the temple, followed by the vizier and other officials. Ipy is thrilled to see a couple of scribes in the group. He recognizes them by the scribe's kit they each carry, with pens, palette, and ink pot.

The queen sits on a throne near the temple gate. The pharaoh prays for a minute then takes off his robe and starts to run around the temple and the chapels that have been set up outside for the festival. While he runs, priests chant prayers for his health and vigor. When he has completed his run, the pharaoh walks up the steps to a throne near the queen. The priests put his robe back on him, and then place the great double crown of Upper and Lower Egypt on his head. The crowd cheers wildly. Now their pharaoh is full of strength and energy and will protect them for another thirty years!

SED FESTIVAL

One of the biggest festivals in Egypt was the **sed** or jubilee festival, held on the thirtieth anniversary of the pharaoh's coronation. The sed festival was a religious ceremony to bring about the pharaoh's rebirth. The pharaoh traveled by boat from temple to temple. At each temple the priests and priestesses prayed that their gods would make the pharaoh as youthfully energetic and healthy as he had been at his coronation. The people hoped that this would keep the pharaoh strong enough to continue ruling for many more years.

ACTIVITY
WHITE CROWN

In this activity you can make the white crown of Upper Egypt. Wear it alone or with the red crown you can make in the next activity.

MATERIALS

newspaper
9-inch (23-cm) balloon
duct tape
scissors
bowl
½ cup (12 cl) of white glue
½ cup (12 cl) of water
spoon
4 double sheets of newspaper
white poster paint
brush
water jar

1. Spread newspaper over your work space.

2. Blow up the balloon, and tie it off.

3. Cut three 6-inch (15-cm) strips of duct tape. Squeeze the end of the balloon between your fingers to make it narrower. Wrap the tape strips around the end of the balloon, as shown below.

4. Pour the glue and water into the bowl, and stir with the spoon till mixed.

5. Tear the newspaper into narrow strips. Dip each strip in the glue mix and wrap it around the balloon in layers, starting at the top of the balloon. Continue until you have covered two thirds of the balloon. Let dry for two days.

6. Pop the balloon. Paint the crown white.

7. When the paint is dry, wear your white crown alone or inside the red crown.

ACTIVITY

RED CROWN

In this activity you can make the red crown of Lower Egypt. Wear it alone, or with the white crown.

MATERIALS

newspaper
28-by-12-inch (70-by-30-cm) piece of red poster board
scissors
yardstick or meterstick
pencil
white glue
stapler

PHARAOH'S CROWN

The pharaoh wore different crowns for different ceremonies. For ordinary occasions he wore a striped cloth scarf with a gold uraeus (cobra) on the front. In Lower Egypt he wore a red crown with a tall peak at the back. In Upper Egypt he wore a conical white crown. For special occasions the pharaoh wore a double crown that combined the red crown and the white crown.

1. Spread the newspaper over your work space.

2. Wrap the poster board around the top of your head. On the inside, mark where the end overlaps. Add 3½ inches (8.75 cm), and cut off any excess.

3. Measure 3½ inches in from each side of the poster board and mark points A, B, C, and D as shown. Rule lines connecting A with B and C with D.

4. Measure 3½ inches up from the bottom on each side of the poster board and mark points E and F. Rule a horizontal line connecting E and F.

5. Measure 6 inches in from where lines A-B and C-D cross line E-F. Mark these points G and H, as shown, and rule lines connecting point A to G and point C to H. Cut out trapezoid A-G-H-C.

6. Fold the poster board in a circle, overlapping the tall ends, with the red side showing. Staple the ends of the crown together. Now wear your crown as pharaoh of Lower Egypt!

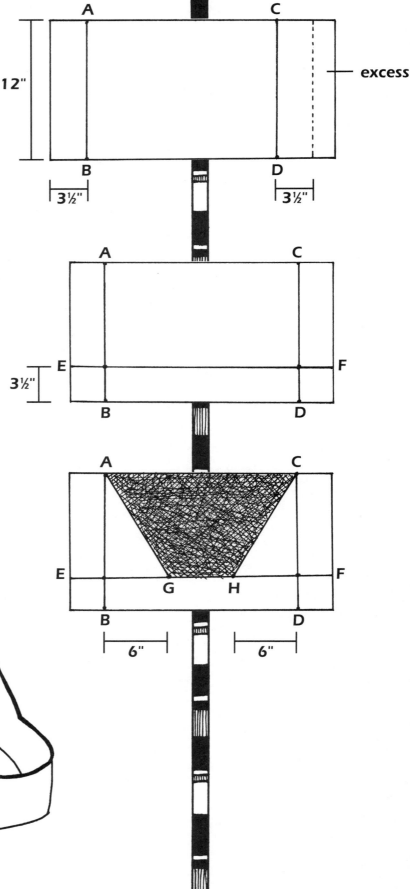

12"

excess

3½"   3½"

A   C

B   D

E   F

3½"

A   C

E   F

G   H

B   D

6"   6"

ACTIVITY

HEADDRESS WITH WADJYT OR NEKHBET ORNAMENT

The royalty of Egypt often wore a narrow band of gold on their heads with a *uraeus*, a representation of the cobra goddess Wadjyt or the vulture goddess Nekhbet, on the front to protect them. Wear your headdress decorated with the image of one of these godesses!

MATERIALS

3-by-6-inch (8.75-by-15-cm) piece of yellow poster board
pencil
colored markers
scissors
stapler
24-by-2-inch (60-by-5-cm) piece of yellow poster board
6 gold-colored rosettes or fancy buttons, 1-inch (2.5-cm) diameter
white glue
3 drinking straws
12-by-6-inch (30-by-15-cm) piece of gold-colored or aluminum foil
masking tape or duct tape

1. On the 3-by-6-inch (8.75-by-15-cm) piece of yellow poster board, draw the uraeus image of Wadjyt or Nekhbet shown below. Color your picture with the markers, then cut it out.

Nehkbet   **Wadjyt**

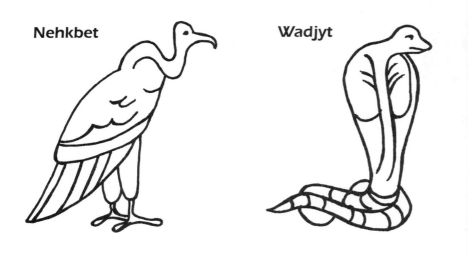

TUTANKHAMUN, BOY PHARAOH

Tutankhamun became pharaoh when he was only nine. The young pharaoh died at age nineteen, in 1323 B.C., and was buried in the Valley of the Kings. Unlike the tombs of other pharaohs, Tutankhamun's tomb remained undisturbed until 1922, when it was discovered by the archaeologists Howard Carter and Lord Caernarvon. It contained Tutankhamun's mummy in a gold coffin with a gold face mask, a gold-covered throne, a chariot, furniture, and everything else the young king needed for the afterlife.

2. Staple the picture to the center of the 24-inch (60-cm) strip of poster board. Glue the rosettes along the sides.

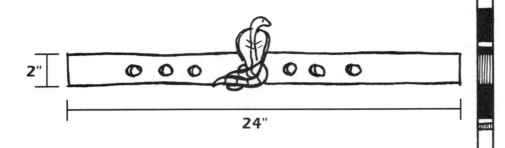

3. Measure the strip of poster board around your head. Staple the ends together. Cut off any excess.

4. Cut the straws into nine equal lengths. Cut the foil into nine pieces 1¼ by 6 inches (3 by 15 cm). Wrap each piece of straw in foil, fastened with a small piece of tape.

5. Pull some of your hair through each piece of straw. Wear your headdress and look like a pharaoh or a queen!

ACTIVITY

PHARAOH'S BEARD

When we see bearded men in Egyptian art, we know they are always foreigners because the ancient Egyptians didn't let their beards grow. But for ceremonies, the pharaohs always wore a false beard braided with gold thread. In Egyptian art you can usually see the hooks that hold the beards on the pharaohs' ears. In this activity, make a false beard and wear it as part of your royal regalia.

MATERIALS

plain paper cup
pencil
paints
brush
water jar
paper hole punch
4-foot (1.3-m) cord
scissors

1. Paint the design shown here on the paper cup.

2. Punch a hole ½ inch (1.25 cm) down from the top. Punch another hole ½ inch (1.25 cm) down from the top on the opposite side.

HATHSHEPSUT, FEMALE PHARAOH

Hathshepsut (ruled 1473–1458 B.C.) was the daughter of Pharaoh Tuthmosis I and wife of Pharaoh Tuthmosis II, with whom she had a daughter but no son. When Hathshepsut's husband died, the next pharaoh should have been his young son by another wife. Hathshepsut thought this was unfair and announced that she would rule with the little boy as coregent. Soon she decided to seize power and become the pharaoh herself.

Hathshepsut built a grand temple at Deir el-Bahri, which included a stone sphinx with her face on it. Since the pharaoh wore a false beard for special occasions, there is a beard hanging down under the sphinx's chin. Later pharaohs disapproved of a female pharaoh and removed Hathshepsut's name from most royal records.

3. Cut the cord in half. Pull one end of each piece through one of the holes, and knot it. Hold the cup on your chin, and pull the ends of the cords around your ears. Knot the cord together. Cut off any extra cord.

ACTIVITY

QUEEN'S HEADDRESS

More than three thousand years ago the sculptor Tuthmose carved a limestone portrait of Queen Nefertiti wearing a black headdress decorated with gold and colorful bands. People today regard this sculpture as one of the most beautiful heads ever carved. Make a copy of the queen's headdress in this activity.

MATERIALS
28-by-12-inch (70-by-30-cm) piece of black poster board
pencil
yardstick or meterstick
scissors
stapler
2 feet (60 cm) of gold braid
3 feet (90 cm) of colorful ribbon
fabric glue or white glue

1. Wrap the poster board around your head. Mark on the inside where the ends overlap. Allow 2 inches (5 cm) of overlap. Cut off any excess.

2. Measure 8 inches (20 cm) up one short side of the poster board, and mark this point A. Rule 8 inches (20 cm) up the other short side, and mark this point B. Use the yardstick or meterstick to find the center point between points A and B, and mark this point C. Measure up 4 inches (30 cm) from point C, to point D. Rule a line connecting points A and D, and points B and D. Cut along these lines.

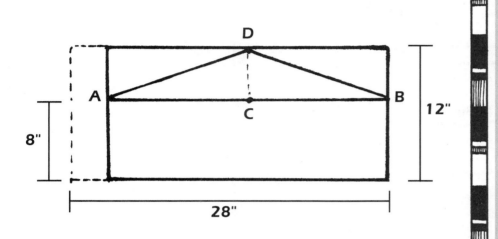

3. Find the center point of the gold braid, and staple it to the headdress at point C. Staple the rest of the braid along the edge of the headdress. Squeeze a thin line of glue along the back of the ribbon. Find the center point of the ribbon, and place it on the center front of the headdress at point C.

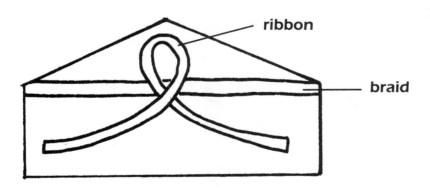

ribbon

braid

NEFERTITI AND AMENOPHIS IV

Queen Nefertiti was married to Pharaoh Amenophis IV, who ruled from 1353 to 1335 B.C. They are remembered because of the beautiful art in their palace and temple at el-Amarna and in the temple of Aten at Karnak. Amenophis IV was not a popular pharaoh. He announced that he would no longer worship all the old gods of Egypt but would worship only the sun god Aten. Amenophis took the new name Akhenaten in honor of Aten. He closed many temples of the other gods, greatly angering the priests and the people.

4. Press the rest of the ribbon on the headdress, crossing it over in the back, as shown in the illustration.

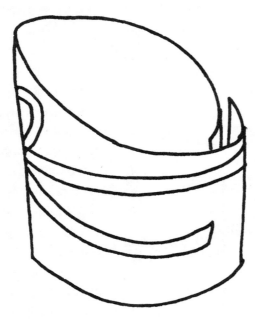

5. Now wear your headdress like a queen!

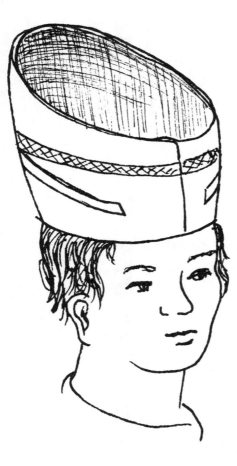

CHAPTER 10

FEASTING ON THE BANKS OF THE NILE

After the great thrill of seeing the pharaoh, Ipy and Meryt have another treat to enjoy—the feast that Neferure and Tutu have been cooking for days! Big baskets of food and jars of beer and wine are keeping cool under the canopy in their boat. Pashed and Tutu put out stools for Paneb and Neferure to sit on, and they bring out a small table for the food. They put cushions on the ground for Ipy and Meryt. The family is glad to sit.

While Tutu and Pashed are setting out the dinner, Paneb pours a cool drink for Neferure and himself. Ipy fans his parents with the palm-leaf fan. Meryt takes out fragrant lotus flowers that she has brought in the boat and ties them into wreaths. She makes a wreath for each of her parents and puts it on their heads. They talk and laugh about the day, enjoying the breeze that is blowing along the Nile, as the beautiful temple glows in the setting sun.

Yogurt with Sliced Cucumber

Egyptians had large herds of cattle. They also farmed goats and sheep and made yogurt and cheese from all these animals' milk. This appetizer serves four people.

INGREDIENTS
4 small cartons or 1 quart (1 l) of plain yogurt
1 small cucumber

TOOLS
4 small bowls
4 small plates
sharp knife

1. Pour a carton of yogurt into each bowl or, if you are using a large container of yogurt, divide the yogurt equally among four small bowls. Put a plate under each bowl.

2. Cut the cucumber into thin slices. Put one quarter of the cucumber slices on each plate.

3. Dip the cucumber slices in the yogurt.

ACTIVITY

HUMMUS WITH FLAT BREAD

Hummus is a spread made from chickpeas or garbanzo beans mixed with vegetable oil. Since the ancient Egyptians had no olive oil, they moistened the spread with sesame seed oil and served it as an appetizer.

This recipe serves four people.

INGREDIENTS
½ cup (0.12 l) of hummus
loaf of pita or other bread

TOOLS
spoon
small bowl
large plate

EGYPTIAN FOODS

When we think of foods from the southern Mediterranean we think of olives, lemons, and tomatoes. But the ancient Egyptians of the Old Kingdom had none of these. Olives and lemons were introduced by the Hyksos, invaders who attacked Egypt around 1700 B.C. (Tomatoes came much later. They were brought from America and were not eaten anywhere before the nineteenth century as they were thought to be poisonous!)

The diet of most Old Kingdom Egyptians consisted mainly of bread, vegetables, eggs, and fruit—a very healthy diet. Favorite vegetables were beans and **melokhia**, a green leafy plant like spinach. They did not have rich gravy or sauces, but flavored foods with herbs—dill, mint, cumin, and parsley—and onions and garlic. Meat was expensive and was rarely eaten except on holidays and at feasts.

1. Spoon the hummus into the bowl. Place the bowl in the middle of the large plate.

2. Break the bread into small, triangle-shaped pieces and put them around the bowl of hummus.

3. Now dip the bread in the hummus, and enjoy!

ACTIVITY

FUL MEDAMES AND EGGS

Ful medames (FOOL muh-DAH-mez), or broad beans, are still popular in Egypt. They are eaten as a main course at breakfast or lunch, or as an appetizer at dinner. They are often served with hard-boiled eggs. It takes a long time to cook dried beans, so start soaking the beans the evening before you will eat them.

This appetizer serves four people.

INGREDIENTS
1 pound (500 g) of dried ful or brown fava beans
4 cloves of garlic
water
4 eggs
2 tablespoons (30 ml) of vegetable oil
sprig of parsley
salt
pepper
cumin

TOOLS

colander
large pot with tight-fitting lid
garlic press
small pot
tablespoon
serving bowl
sharp knife
adult helper for using the stove and knife

1. Rinse the beans in the colander under the cold-water faucet.

2. Put the beans in the pot, and cover with cold water. Soak them for eight hours.

3. Drain the beans, then cover them with fresh water. Ask your adult helper to put the pot on the stove and bring the water to a boil. Cover and simmer for four to six hours, until the beans are tender.

4. Put the eggs in the small pot. Cover with cold water. Ask your adult helper to turn the stove on, and bring the eggs to a boil. Boil for ten minutes, then drain. When the eggs are cool, peel and slice them.

5. Press the garlic. Ask your helper to chop the parsley.

6. When the beans are tender, drain. Toss with garlic. Add salt, pepper, and cumin to taste.

7. Serve the beans in a bowl, topped with the eggs. Sprinkle parsley on top.

KEEPING FOOD FRESH IN EGYPT

The Egyptians had no refrigerators or freezers! It was hard for them to keep food fresh in their hot climate. They could only preserve food by drying it, or salting it, or pickling it. They also made foods last longer by changing perishable foods into longer-lasting foods—for example, by making bread into beer, fruit into wine, and milk into yogurt or cheese.

After the family members have all nibbled on the appetizers, Meryt brings out her harp and sings while Tutu dances. They all sway to the music. As the main course is put on the table, Paneb calls on them to offer up a prayer in thanks to the goddesses Bastet and Hathor, and for the pharaoh's good health. They hold up their cups and pour a little drink on the ground as an offering to the goddesses.

ACTIVITY

CHICKEN STEW WITH MELOKHIA

On festive days, Egyptians enjoyed eating meat with their vegetables. They cooked it by boiling or roasting. If you can't find *melokhia,* use spinach or chard to make this stew.

This main dish serves four people.

INGREDIENTS

2 boneless, skinless chicken breasts
salt
pepper
1 cup (250 ml) of chicken broth
1 quart (1 l) of water
3 cups (0.45 kg) of fresh lima beans
1 garlic bulb
3 onions
melokhia, chard, or spinach
sprig of parsley

TOOLS

large cooking pot
skimmer or large spoon

sharp knife
garlic press
serving bowl and spoon
adult helper

1. Sprinkle salt and pepper on the chicken. Put the chicken, chicken broth, and water into the pot. Ask your helper to turn the stove on, and bring the pot to a boil. Boil gently for ten minutes. Skim the broth several times as it boils.

2. Take out the chicken and let it cool. Cut it into eight pieces.

3. Peel the garlic. Press the cloves. Chop the onions.

4. Reduce the heat to medium low. Put the chicken, lima beans, onions, and garlic in the pot. Simmer for one hour. Skim frequently.

5. Wash the greens well under the faucet. Tear them into small pieces. Add them to the pot, and simmer them for ten minutes.

6. Chop the parsley. Pour the stew into the serving bowl, and decorate with the parsley.

BREAD AND BEER

Bread was the most important food in Egypt. The Egyptians ate bread made from wheat and barley. They made their bread in several shapes. A common shape was the triangle, and this kind of loaf was called a **ta**. Ta was similar to our modern pita bread. When the bread became stale, the Egyptians mashed it in water, where it was fermented (chemically changed so that its sugar became alcohol) to become beer—the Egyptians' favorite drink. To flavor their beer, they added sweet fruits such as dates.

ACTIVITY
SESAME SEED COOKIES

The Egyptian diet included seeds and nuts, which are good sources of protein. Sweeten these cookies with honey, and serve them with grapes and grape juice

INGREDIENTS

1 cup (250 ml) of vegetable shortening
⅔ cup (167 ml) of honey
2 cups (500 ml) of all-purpose flour
1 cup (250 ml) of whole-wheat flour
1 teaspoon of baking powder
1 teaspoon of salt
6 to 7 tablespoons (100 ml) of water
2 tablespoons (30 ml) of sesame seeds
¼ cup (63 ml) of honey

TOOLS

baking sheet
flour sifter
large mixing bowl
fork
wooden spoon
rolling pin
measuring cup
measuring spoon
cookie cutter
oven mitts
adult helper

1. Preheat the oven to 350 degrees F. Grease the baking sheet.

2. Mix together the shortening and ⅔ cup (167 ml) of honey.

3. Sift the flours, salt, and baking powder together. Use the fork to stir the dry mixture into the shortening.

4. Sprinkle on half of the water. Mold the dough with your hands, adding enough water so that it holds together.

5. Sprinkle a few spoons of flour on your work surface, and roll out the dough until it is ¼ inch (0.6 cm) thick.

6. Stir the seeds and ¼ cup (63 ml) of honey together to make a paste. Spread the paste over the dough. Use the cookie cutter to cut out the cookies, and put them on the baking sheet.

7. Bake for ten minutes, until the edges are lightly browned.

8. Have your adult helper use the oven mitts to take the baking sheet out of the oven.

9. Let the cookies cool for about fifteen minutes before serving.

EGYPTIAN DINING

Egyptians ate bread and many kinds of vegetables for their main course at dinner, and for dessert they enjoyed many kinds of fruit. Dates, figs, grapes, melons, and pomegranates were all popular. They had no sugar, but they loved sweet tastes and sweetened cakes with honey and fruit juice.

Egyptians roasted or boiled their food over an open fire or baked it in a clay oven shaped like a cone or a cylinder. They stored food and drink in clay pots. Most people ate off pottery plates and drank from pottery cups. Rich people ate off gold plates. They used bronze knives and spoons to prepare the food, but then they ate it with their fingers. No forks!

RESOURCES

FOR CHILDREN

Clare, John D., editor. *Pyramids of Egypt*. New York: Harcourt Brace Jovanovich/Gulliver Books, 1992.

Ganeri, Anita. *Pharaohs and Mummies*. New York: Ladybird Books, 1996.

Hart, George. *Ancient Egypt: Exploring the Past*. New York: Harcourt Brace Jovanovich/Gulliver Books, 1988.

Millard, Anne. *Mysteries of the Pyramids*. Brookfield, CT: Copper Beach Books, 1995.

Milton, Joyce. *Mummies*. New York: Grosset and Dunlap, 1996.

FOR ADULTS

Andreu, Guillemette. *Egypt in the Age of the Pyramids*. Ithaca and London: Cornell University Press, 1997.

Grimal, Nicholas. *A History of Ancient Egypt*. Oxford/Malden: Blackwell, 1994.

Robins, Gay. *The Art of Ancient Egypt*. Cambridge, MA: Harvard University Press, 1997.

FOR TEACHERS

Balkwill, Richard. *Food and Feasts in Ancient Egypt*. New York: New Discovery Books, 1994.

Harris, Geraldine. *Ancient Egypt: Cultural Atlas for Young People*. New York: Facts on File, 1990.

Sterling, Mary Ellen. *Thematic Unit: Ancient Egypt*. Huntington Beach, CA: Teacher Created Materials, 1992.

FOR EVERYONE

Friedman, Florence Dunn. *Gifts of the Nile: Ancient Egyptian Faience*. New York: Thames and Hudson, 1998.

Roehrig, Catherine. *Fun with Hieroglyhs*. New York: Metropolitan Museum of Art/Viking, 1990.

GLOSSARY

akhet   flood season

amulet   a charm worn to protect against misfortune

ankh   sign of life

Apis bull   a special live bull believed to represent the god Ptah

Atum   god of creation and the sun

bay   palm stick

benben   a pyramid-shape stone in the temple of Re at Heliopolis, which the Egyptians believed was the place where the world was created

capstone   topmost stone of a pyramid

cartouche   an oval line enclosing the name of a pharaoh in hieroglyphic writing

Delta   the marshy land around the mouth of the Nile River

Deshret   Red Land in ancient Egypt

djed   an amulet representing the spine of the god Osiris

felucca   a Nile sailboat

Geb   god of the earth

Heliopolis   city near Memphis

hieroglyph   Egyptian picture writing

jubilee   anniversary

Kemet   Black Land in ancient Egypt

lapis lazuli   blue gemstone

ma'at   goodness, order, the will of the gods

Ma'at   goddess of truth

mastaba   a bench, or a benchlike tomb

menat   a string of beads shaken as a musical instrument

mortuary temple   a temple built near a pyramid where the pharaoh's body was mummified

mummify   to preserve a body by drying it out

mummiya   Arabic for "bitumen," which people thought the Egyptians used to mummify bodies

mummy   a body preserved by drying

Nut   goddess of the sky

ostrakon   Greek word for a small piece of clay used for writing on

peret   "coming forth," planting season

pharaoh   the king of ancient Egypt

Ptah   god of creation and of crafts; shown as a mummified man

pylon   slanting, angular pillar at the entrance to an Egyptian temple

Rameses II   a pharaoh who ruled from 1292 to 1225 B.C. and built many temples

Re   god of the sun, shown as a man with a falcon's head and a sun disk headdress; also spelled Ra

scarab   image of the dung beetle, worn as an amulet

sed   festival of the pharaoh's jubilee

Serapeum   great underground tomb at Saqqara, where the Apis bulls were buried

shabti (or ushabti)   models of servants placed in the pharaohs' tombs

shemu   drought season

Shu   god of air

sistrum   a rattle used as a musical instrument

ta   a loaf of bread shaped like a triangle

Tefnut   goddess of water

turquoise   blue-green gemstone

INDEX

embalming, 37, 47

Ethiopia, 1

F

face-painting activity, 68–69

family names, 2

farming, 1

felucca (boat), 59

festival, 5

flooding of the Nile, 1,
16–17, 22

flute, 25

food, 56, 64, 97–105

 Hummus with Flat Bread,
  99–100

 Yogurt with Sliced
  Cucumber, 98–99

 Ful Medames and Eggs,
  100–101

 Chicken Stew with
  Melokhia, 102–103

 Sesame Seed Cookies, 104–
  105

ful medames (broad beans),
 100

funeral, 46

furniture, 11, 37

G

games, 25, 64

 senet game activity, 25–29

 serpent game activity, 64–66

Giza (place), 1–2, 17–18, 47

gods of Egypt, 13

Great Pyramid, 2, 17

H

harp, 24–25, 29, 80

Hathor (cow goddess), 13,
78, 79, 81, 102

 Hathor headdress activity,
  78–80

Hathshepsut (pharaoh), 93

headdress activities

 Hathor headdress, 78–80

 Nefertiti headdress, 94–96

 perfume cone, 69–70

 red crown, 89–90

 Wadjyt or Nekhbet head-
  dress, 91–92

 white crown, 88–89

Heliopolis (place), 45

hieroglyph (Egyptian picture
 writing), 18, 28, 38–39,
 41, 45

 activity, 38–39

hippopotamus goddess, 61

hippopotamus statue activity,
 61–63

Horus (hawk form of the sun
 god), 13

house, 3, 24–25

House of Life (scribes'
 school), 36–38

Hyksos (nation), 99

I

Imhotep, 19

Isis (goddess), 29

J

jewelry, 13, 75

 ankh amulet activity, 9–11

 armlet activity, 75

 broad collar activity, 70–74

 scarab activity, 13–15

jubilee, 2, 76, 86-87

SPEND THE DAY
IN ANCIENT EGYPT